SECURITY IN THE PERSIAN GULF I

The International Institute for Strategic Studies was founded in 1958 as a centre for the provision of information on and research into the problems of international security, defence and arms control in the nuclear age. It is international in its Council and staff, and its membership is drawn from over fifty countries. It is independent of governments and is not the advocate of any particular interest.

The Institute is concerned with strategic questions – not just with the military aspects of security but with the social and economic sources and political and moral implications of the use and existence of armed force: in other words, with the basic problems of peace.

The Institute's publications are intended for a much wider audience than its own membership and are available to the general public on special subscription terms or singly.

Security in the Persian Gulf I:

Domestic Political Factors

Edited by

SHAHRAM CHUBIN

Regional Security Co-ordinator,
International Institute for Strategic Studies

Published for
THE INTERNATIONAL INSTITUTE
FOR STRATEGIC STUDIES
by
ALLANHELD, OSMUN

Published in the United States of America in 1981 by

Allanheld, Osmun & Co. Publishers, Inc.,
6 South Fullerton Avenue, Montclair, New Jersey 07042.

Printed in Great Britain

ISBN 0-86598-044-6

Contents

Contributors

John Duke Anthony	:	Professor at School for Advanced International Studies (SAIS) John Hopkins University, Washington DC
Michael Field	:	Freelance writer formerly with the *Financial Times*
Allan G. Hill	:	Senior Research Fellow London School of Hygiene and Tropical Medicine
Arnold Hottinger	:	Correspondent for the *Neue Zuricher* *Zeitung*, Zurich

Contributors

Introduction
Shahram Chubin

These papers were originally presented at an international conference in November 1979. They have been amended in the light of conference discussions as well as subsequent events.

The Institute has embarked on a major study of security in the Gulf. These conference topics were intended to serve as a launching point for the wider project, but were consciously framed to address the dynamics of political forces inside the littoral states. It may appear in the light of the Soviet invasion of Afghanistan, and of developments in Iran, which have concentrated superpower attention on this region, that this is too narrow a focus. I do not believe that this is the case. In the Gulf threats to security come from many sources. For the foreseeable future—for the next decade at least—OECD dependency will continue (if it does not increase) on the Gulf for oil supplies, for 40 per cent of world oil is located here. Although a common interest, Alliance members have differential dependencies and vulnerabilities. Soviet interest in the region has also grown as the Soviet Union has acquired most of the attributes of a global power, and that interest may increase in the 1980s with the need to secure oil for Eastern Europe and possibly a direct need for oil imports to the Soviet Union.

Together with a growing and overlapping interest by the superpowers there has occurred a shift in the military balance of power in the region. This is in part a consequence of Britain's winding down of imperial commitment and American reluctance to substitute for it; in part a result of growing Soviet military power; and in part an outgrowth of the regional political environment in which local states are more assertive about their own priorities, goals and interests. The military imbalance—

reflecting geopolitical asymmetries—has not yet had a decisive effect on the politics of the region but on the level of political perceptions it has a marked and (presumably given the trends) a growing one. The challenge for the two blocs in the next decade will be to work out rules of engagement that protect their interests but do not unduly disturb their existing relationships with regional states. A major obstacle to such an agreement on mutual access is likely to be the unstable regional political environment which will provide tempting opportunities for the exploitation and enhancement of one side's interests, whilst administering a setback to the other. The test will be to devise a sufficiently discriminating policy that will be able both to distinguish between and to address separately instabilities that have regional origins and instabilities that are clear threats to Western interests fostered by the opposing bloc.

For the West, dependency on the Persian Gulf extends beyond the mere flow of oil. The issues of price and rate of production are also important. The notion that oil producing states cannot 'drink their oil' has been disproved by recent history; for the producer, limiting production can be a very economical way of raising prices. The foreign orientation of the producing states is therefore of consequence; policy changes can affect the oil flow. If oil embargoes (or reduced production) are one possibility, another is interruption from loss of control. Revolutions (as in Iran), or major inter-state warfare illustrate this.

For better or worse, therefore, the economic and political wellbeing of the OECD will be progressively entangled with the destiny of the Gulf states. Yet this region is unlike any other in which the West has vital security interests. It is not, and cannot be, covered by a traditional security guarantee—like NATO. It is culturally separate. It is undergoing a period of rapid change which creates strains on existing societies and forms of government whose ultimate shape is of necessity uncertain. These three elements in combination underscore the delicacy of the relationship between the West and the oil producers. Regional politics prevent an alliance with the West because of the West's support for Israel. The cultural divide inhibits an intimate relationship and the stresses of 'modernization' make a sound analysis of the region's 'stability' difficult.

Despite the military 'overhang' problem and superpower rivalry, the major threats to the region are only partly external. Inter-state rivalries and conflicts arising from ideological, dynastic or historical and territorial differences are another—and fertile—source of instability. More important still are the range of forces unleashed by the rapid embrace of new technology and new ideas, made possible by oil wealth.

What then are the local instabilities and are they evenly distributed? The conference papers look at their domestic origins and focus on the differences among the least studied states. Iran and Iraq have been excluded on the grounds that they are already relatively well studied.

Their collective aim is to identify various aspects of the modernization process, economic development, the politicization of populations, and urbanization, and to discuss their varying impact on the Gulf states, with reference to their (indigenous) capacity to deal with them. The question of the adaptability of existing institutions (formal and informal) and procedures is thus addressed.

The challenges faced by the states are broadly comparable:

1 Rapid rates of population growth with a large proportion of restive young.

2 Movement from rural areas into towns and cities which entails urbanization, and the decline of traditional society, etc.

3 The adaptation of political institutions to the need for more political participation.

4 The diversification of economies away from a single resource.

5 Manpower shortages, immigrants and their political implications.

6 The reconciliation and synthesis of traditional moral values with new norms and social organization.

In addressing these and other questions, two papers are organized around specific countries and two along functional lines. The first two compare political forces at work in Saudi Arabia, Kuwait, Bahrain and the UAE; the latter two discuss the problems of states endowed with adequate but finite material resources, but lacking human and other requisites for their optimum use. The Gulf states are all clearly undergoing a similar process and face parallel predicaments but neither the pressures nor their means for coping with them are identical. This is the result of different social structures and political institutions and an outgrowth of differential oil income. Bahrain, one of the earliest and now a declining oil producer, was perhaps least affected by the price explosion of the 1970s; it has now lived with an urban and relatively politicized population for two decades. Bahrain is also less affected by immigrant populations which Kutait and Saudi Arabia witness in different forms. Similarly, economic development has had differential impact on Kuwait and Saudi Arabia; the former has managed the task of distribution better than the latter where a major cleavage exists (according to Arnold Hottinger) between the small stratum of very rich and the majority, very poor.

In the UAE the problems are different as John Duke Anthony shows. The federation of seven unequally endowed shaikhdoms has lasted a decade and survived periodic crises. In practice, rivalries have persisted in the distribution of key portfolios, in differences in the pace and degree of integration and especially in the composition and control of the union versus the individual shaikhly armed forces. Rivalry also persists in the tendency toward the competition in prestige projects rather than in a rationalized co-ordination of industrialization. The UAE has survived despite inequalities in wealth, traditional rivalries, and reliance on foreign immigrants; three-quarters of the population are foreigners (mainly non-Arabs; Indians, Pakistanis, Iranians and Baluchis). Differences between the two core states—Dubai and Abu Dhabi—reflect historical rivalries but these have nevertheless been submerged enough to allow the union to survive.

Policies which have encouraged the spreading of wealth among the emirates have given the union a stronger foundation. Saudi Arabia, the most influential outside power, has lent its support to this. As a result the UAE appears more stable than the more homogenous Saudi Arabia.

The modernization process is inherently stressful; the leadership embarks upon a path whose destination is uncertain. It loosens its bonds with its traditional constituency in the expectation of receiving support and loyalty from the new, transformed, populace. In so doing it runs the risk of alienating its power base without compensating gains elsewhere. As in Iran, for diametrically opposed reasons, the left and right might become dissatisfied and unite to replace the government, in the guise of a 'traditional backlash'.

The economic 'problems' of oil rich states may be much more serious than they are conspicuous. Oil revenues distort economic development in a profound way. Oil revenues serve to cover and hence foster mistakes. They encourage a fundamental attitude toward planning that lacks measurable criteria, that is uneconomic, and which promotes wastefulness and 'white elephants'. To be sure, oil revenues are a great asset and Michael Field's somewhat optimistic paper describes the economic benefits associated with them. If states suffer from small markets, small or a poorly trained labour pool or inadequate infrastructure, these can be rectified by oil revenues. States can provide a complete spectrum of services to their citizens—free education and health care, food and housing subsidies and no taxes. But the political costs of such policies are perhaps less obvious. As Allan Hill notes, the importation of labour creates its own problems. Immigrants are discriminated against. Whether emboldened or thoroughly alienated they pose potential political problems for they may combine to further 'their interests at the expense of the host country'. In some states the proportion of the population that are native citizens is less than half—as in Kuwait and the UAE. In others, such as Saudi Arabia, they are the dominant element in the workforce. According to some calculations, the number of immigrants in the Gulf will number five million by 1985 (as against three million in 1980). The political consequences of this will vary but almost everywhere a two class system will be perpetuated differentiating in favour of the native citizens and against the often more productive immigrant.

Michael Field's paper strengthens the case for those who argue that while an economic opportunity exists—and a unique one among less developed countries—oil revenues are as much a political liability as an economic asset. The welfare state and rentier mentality create economic problems in the longer run when citizens see the state's task as one of providing them with benefits but with little commensurate responsibility of their own. But it also creates political problems for governments which are burdened with demands that they can scarcely be expected to bear. The purely financial consequences of the enrichment mentality which may encourage corruption and speculation may not be totally without value; it may, for example, assist in the spreading of wealth. Again, politically, the costs are high as materialism—and the social disruption attendant on rapid change—comes to be seen as an alien, intrusive force.

A further problem is created by surplus income and its productive use. Invested locally it tends after a certain point to strain the infrastructure and increase inflation. Invested overseas it is protected against neither inflation nor seizure. The economic incentives for conserving oil production appear to be strong and growing. This reinforces other conclusions: that problems arise not from too little but from too much growth; that rapid change increases inequalities; and that the process of modernization is inherently unpredictable in its outcome. The risks of not moving on the political front, however, may be higher in the storing up of tensions. In Bahrain and Kuwait there have been indications of an interest in reviving the limited constitutional experiments, the National Assemblies that were dissolved in 1975 and 1976. Even in Saudi Arabia, long opposed to these experiments, there is a new urgency since the November Mecca Mosque episode of creating a Consultative Council. Iraq too, although not the subject of this study, is also, in mid 1980, moving towards elections. Few societies can absorb the massive concentrated infusion of money without consequent strains on their value systems, pattern of social organization and resultant stability. Yet from the Western viewpoint the overriding need is for an orderly 'process' of development that leaves intact those mechanisms most conducive to the management of the transition. If it is not to be disruptive and disorderly, it will require a degree of continuity with past experience and the retention of the authentically valuable rather than indiscriminate acceptance of change for its own sake.

For the West, the 'security of oil supplies' has tended to have a circumscribed meaning unrelated to its political context. The extraordinary social and political pressures released by the wrenching of the states of the Gulf from their traditional patterns of existence has immensely complicated their governance. To these, as the region's geopolitical importance has risen, regional and external pressures have been added. An understanding of these pressures is the first step toward a policy that can be responsive to them.

As the West's interest in the Persian Gulf has shifted from denying the region to the USSR to securing access to the flow of oil on acceptable terms, the purely military dimension of her influence has declined. As part of this project a separate paper on the Limitations and Scope of outside Power Influence will be forthcoming. Increased dependence has been occurring at a time of decreased influence. Internal instabilities are only one of several sources of threat to the security of oil supplies and they are perhaps the least amenable to Western influence. The others are: superpower rivalry; local conflicts; terrorist activities and regional political pressures. Nevertheless, given the multiple threats to its interests, the West has had to become more entangled in the affairs of the Gulf. The challenge for the West will be in defining security in a region where stability is precarious. Although limited, Western power is not inconsequential. At the least it should demonstrate more sensitivity to regional politics and local priorities and avoid exacerbating existing instabilities—by unbridled commercialism, for example. More positively, the power that appears militarily dependable and genuinely committed to the region's welfare will be in a position to benefit. It may not influence events directly but it will influence—through the perceptions of local states—their choices as they weigh the balance of risks involved in potential policies.

1 Political institutions in Saudi Arabia, Kuwait and Bahrain

Arnold Hottinger

The leadership tradition in the Arab world

The governments of Kuwait, Bahrain and Saudi Arabia have all grown out of what can be termed the Arab tribal tradition of government. This is characterised by the rule of one man, a shaikh, usually tempered by some kind of informal mechanism of consultation, a tribal council. The shaikh or ruler can be 'elected' but this is no formal election—rather a *de facto* nomination arrived at by a process of internal struggles, alliances and consultations which eventually leads to the most powerful, rich, prestigious and influential head of clan becoming tribal boss. Once firmly entrenched, there is a tendency for the leader to keep the position within his clan and family. This is often possible because the shaikh or ruler can use his position to further increase his pre-eminent standing by gaining more riches, prestige, influence, etc. over other possible rivals.

A change of ruling clan and family usually occurs if the shaikh fails in his undertakings. In that case his prestige is diminished and possible rivals are given a chance to replace him. They will normally belong to a different clan or even tribe because the disaster befalling the previous shaikh is normally of a collective nature such as defeat in a tribal war. This invariably means that the whole clan or tribe loses power thus allowing a new clan or tribe to take over the leadership.

No hereditary rule

If there is no disaster, the leadership will remain within the ruling

1

family—but it is not a hereditary leadership. Children or even young men cannot lead a clan or tribe. The leadership usually then goes to some relative of the previous ruler, and the family council speaks an authoritative word when the decision is made. The deceased ruler or shaikh, particularly if he has been powerful and successful, may also indicate the choice of his successor, frequently by associating him with his rule while he still remains the supreme authority. Money and other forms of fortune also play an important part in achieving and maintaining rule. The classical tribal shaikh has to be rich enough to offer lavish hospitality to his followers and to outside dignitaries. He is also a war leader and obtains an important part of the spoils of war. But essentially he remains *primus inter pares,* and a symbol of this position is the fact that all tribal subjects or colleagues—both qualifications apply—have free access to the shaikh and can come to him to present grievances or requests either at any time or, if the standing of the ruler increases, at certain hours in the evening when a *Majlis* is held.

Titulation

A major tribal leader is given the title *amir,* commander, and this is the title officially translated as 'ruler' which is still held by those who rule Kuwait and Bahrain. The passage between shaikh and amir is fluid (as are most things within this traditional concept of tribal leadership); in current language, but not in official titulation, both rulers are still known as the shaikh. *Malik,* or 'king', which has been the title of the ruler of Saudi Arabia since Malik Abdul Aziz Ibn Sa'ud, implies a greater distance between the ruler and the ruled. However, it is not really a Bedouin title and it can even imply a negative shade of meaning, denoting a 'foreign' ruler from the city tradition of non-desert lands. It is not precisely clear when Abdul Aziz assumed the title of Malik, but it was probably when he started preparing the conquest of Mecca and came into competition with the other *Muluk* (kings) created by the colonial powers, basically Great Britain. Abdul Aziz could not afford to be inferior to his rival 'king' Hussain, the Sharif of Mecca, or later his sons Faisal, the 'king' of Iraq and Abdullah, 'king' of Jordan.

It is evident that many of the characteristics of this traditional tribal leadership concept have remained in all three countries. They were only slightly modified as they emerged as rich, very rich or immensely rich oil states and began affording themselves cities and more or less modern economies, development plans, bureaucrats, welfare institutions, schools and universities, standing armies, air forces, overseas representatives, immigrant populations and so forth.

From clan to government

The different members of the ruler's family in all three countries took over the newly formed ministries, particularly the key ones of finance, security (internally and externally), sometimes oil, sometimes foreign affairs, and almost always inter-Arab relations. Technicians were recruited to run those ministries under 'Royal' direction. In some less sensitive and more technical ministries and state agencies so-called commoners, i.e. people who did not belong to the ruling families, were used as ministers, particularly when technicians were needed.

Many of the other institutions remained. The ruler, or amir, consulted with his family when important decisions had to be taken or appointments made. Part of the state income went into his private treasury from which his own expenses and many of the necessary prestige payments were met. Budgets were introduced in order to administer the rest of the state money. In Bahrain a fixed proportion of the state income, one quarter (which in 1975 equalled seven million dollars), goes to the family, and the internal distribution of that money is decided by the ruler and his informal family council. Similar flexible rules or division apply in the other two states, but the amounts are, of course, much more substantial. The *Majlis* with theoretical free access for all 'subjects' has remained, although in a rudimentary, formalized way. The principle of heredity has not been introduced, and the succession is still managed by the former ruler and the family council. It has been stabilized to some degree by introducing the concept of successor to the 'throne' who, in all three countries, is given the office of prime minister, and who is generally recognized as the heir. But until the actual succession takes place there is always the possibility of upset.

The flexibility of one man rule

In all these three countries the government structures have changed much less than their economic and social features. The latter have been changed by oil and oil money, and subsequently by the amenities which those riches brought—hospitals, schools, building activities encompassing whole cities and a totally new infrastructure for the entire country in each case. The nature of the leadership, particularly at the highest level, has remained essentially unchanged since Bedouin times, although it has been expanded enormously in the middle and lower tiers by the creation of large bureaucracies. The fact that the type of top leadership could be preserved shows the flexibility and adaptability of the traditional system of tribal rule. The simplicity of the system has proved as adaptable as the members of the top family themselves, limited only by their ability to learn to adapt themselves to the new circumstances.

Removal of unfit rulers

There have been some failures in learning; the most notable example was that of King Sa'ud Ibn Abdul Aziz, who increased the sumptious expenses expected from a Bedouin chief in proportion to the growth of his oil income without much consideration for the other needs of the kingdom, from defence to development. In consequence, he spent most of the country's money and his own energy in building expensive palaces and in other conspicuous and unproductive efforts to consume the oil millions. As at the same time Abdel Nasser was making a determined attempt to subvert Saudi Arabia and to bring the royal family down, a crisis developed. It was most dangerous at the period after the fall of the Yemeni *Imam* as a result of an internal revolution strongly sustained by Egyptian troops. The crisis was finally mastered by King Faisal, the second brother of Sa'ud, after the family council had decided that the King had to remit his powers to him and—at a latter stage—deposed the King altogether. This was probably the most severe crisis the Saudi kingdom has so far had to face. Its danger came from the combination of interior weaknesses and exterior, pan-Arab, threat. The shadow of Nasserism hung over the kingdom from 1962, the beginning of the Yemeni war, up to 1967 when the threat disappeared as a result of the defeat of the Egyptians in the Six Day War. At one time, Nasser had even formed a Saudi government-in-exile and some Saudi princes, together with several pilots and their airplanes, defected to him. His frugal standard of living soon helped to rectify the precarious state finances, he appealed to tribal loyalty and he built up the Saudi army and tribal forces (White army). Saudi Arabia fostered countersubversion in the Yemen by aiding the deposed Imam Badr against the pro-Egyptian revolution and appealed for American aid via diplomatic channels. Finally, Faisal promoted a pan-Islamic policy designed to counter the pan-Arab appeal of Nasser and an Arab policy designed to keep Egypt in check by discreetly aiding all enemies of Egypt.

Another conspicuous case of failing to evolve with the times was that of Shaikh Shakhbut of Abu Dhabi, who was unwilling to develop his country as quickly as his new oil fortune would have permitted. He was called a miser and eventually in 1966 was replaced by his more generous brother Zaid in a palace coup aided, if not actually engineered, by the British, at that time the protecting power. A comparable situation arose in Oman where, in 1970, Sultan Said Bin Taimour was deposed (again with British intervention) in favour of his son. Taimour's excessively tyrannical rule was considered especially dangerous in the context of the subversive guerrilla activity initiated by PFLOAG (Peoples Front for the Liberation of Oman and the Arab Gulf—now known as PFLO as its Arab Gulf aspirations have been provisionally suspended), a marxist front aided by revolutionary South Yemen. His son, Sultan Qabus, was able to defeat the rebellion. Said Bin Taimur had been anchored deep in a medieval past and had been incapable of meeting the rising aspirations of his subjects. Similarily, the Amir of Qatar was replaced in 1972

4

by a more 'modern' relative when the family council decided that the old amir no longer met the needs of the day.

The tribal system therefore clearly possesses corrective mechanisms which can be brought into play when the ruling family becomes aware of a collective danger and of the incapacity of the ruling amir to master it. In the past such corrections have naturally been accompanied by violence with the amir often being killed either by a relative or as a result of a conspiracy of relatives. The fact that deposition and exile have now taken the place of physical elimination is partly due to the availability of friendly powers willing to smooth over the process and to provide exile,[1] and also due to the fact that, as in many other aspects of present day social and political life, the availability of large amounts of money helps to 'humanize' this process.

Within the common framework of leadership derived from the traditional system of rule of the tribes, the three countries considered here have had their individual characteristics, diverging fortunes and developments and differing difficulties which in each case have tended to modify the style and details of leadership and rule.

Bahrain

In a sense, Bahrain has gone through the most gradual and least turbulent development due to the fact that oil has been produced for a relatively long time (since 1932) and in relatively small quantities (only 19.9 million barrels a year in 1977 and declining by 4 per cent in recent years). This has meant a modest but steady influx of money into the state treasury and into the amir's personal exchequer (as mentioned above, three-quarters for the state, one quarter for the amir and his family). The relatively small trickle of money combined with the fact that Bahrain had been an urban horticultural community of settled nature for centuries, also aided by sober British supervision of the administration up to 1971, has given rise to the gradual development of the Bahraini community. Initially, oil royalties were used for sanitation, schooling, infrastructure (including housing and security) and the continuity of such investments over the decades has permitted the development of Bahrain as a centre of the service industries for the whole Gulf region. Air transport, communications, a hotel industry and some industrialization were added to the main staple industries of the past—date cultivation, shipbuilding, pearling, commerce, fishing and sea transport.

1 Ex-King Said retired to exile in Cairo and Sultan Taimour found exile in London.

The urban nature of much of Bahrain has meant a quick politicization of the populace and the rather rapid penetration of ideas such as Nasser's pan-Arabism and the Movement of Arab Nationalists (Haraka). This has posed a security threat to the regime. There have been serious riots particularly in times of general pan-Arab agitation, and the Protectorate authorities have taken severe action against actual and potential subversive elements who belonged mostly to the educated and partially educated lower classes. A typical example was the agitation of 1956 (the year of Suez) against the protective power and the ruling house. It was followed by the exile of leading Nasserites and Harakis to Saint Helena (lasting in some cases until 1961), and later, after more trouble, by a permanent state of emergency which lasted from 1961 to 1971 (when independence was granted). But this state of emergency was discreetly managed. It served basically as an instrument to keep the known political opposition under the menace of incarceration. A very tough but apparently capable British police specialist was brought in by the Protectorate authority and was later kept on by the amir in the quality of an adviser to the independent state. He had served before against the Mau Mau insurrection in Kenya. It seems to be principally due to him that the opposition was contained and, with the decline of the general pan-Arab fortunes of Narrerism, of the Haraka and later the PFLOAG mentioned above, the opposition appears to have become rather quiescent.

No viable parliament

In the atmosphere of relatively mild but persistent and systematically managed policy repression it proved impossible to introduce a parliament. This was attempted in 1973 but it was dissolved after twenty months. Saudi Arabia, an influential neighbour of Bahrain, never looked with favour on this experiment, because Riyadh never intended to have a parliament and disliked the precedents created in Bahrain and Kuwait. But a still more decisive reason for the abolition of the assembly was the fact that a vocal minority of deputies began questioning in public the prerogatives of the amir and his family. They had some success among their parliamentary colleagues who had been elected on more conservative tickets, because of the natural tendency of such assemblies to seek to widen and affirm their sovereignty and independence. Thus the interests of the amir and the assembly clashed. The press played its usual role of publicizing and amplifying the claims of the opposition deputies, and the assembly was dissolved. Government continued under the management of different ministers with the key portfolios being retained by the ruling house and the attention of the community was shifted, by a carefully controlled press, onto the essentially technical tasks of development which have become increasingly more complex as the sophistication of the services rendered increased, and ever more

urgent as the oil royalties declined due to the exhaustion of the local
oil wells.

A post-oil economy?

Bahrain has been the first oil state to face the transition from an oil to
a post-oil economy. But this transition has been relatively easy for the
island state. Because the oil revenues were always reasonably limited, a
non-oil economy had always been maintained and was added to over
the years. Moreover, Bahrain can take advantage of the other oil countries
around the Gulf, who are still extraordinarily rich, by offering them its
services. This service role will be much more difficult to build up and
sustain once the revenues of the big oil producers begin to decline.
Being forced to develop its services at a relatively early stage, while there
is still plenty of excess money all over the Gulf, Bahrain will have a
distinct advantage over the purely oil producing countries whose
economies will have to adapt as their revenues begin to decline.

The Shi'i threat

Bahrain has become preoccupied with the Shi'i revolution in Iran, and
the apparent intention of part of the ruling Shi'i establishment there to
'export the revolution', This is hardly surprising when it is remembered
that Iranian claims to sovereignty over the islands were only dropped
by the Shah in 1970.
    In August 1979 about 1,500 Shi'is demonstrated in the bazaar centre
of old Bahrain and such demonstrations were repeated several times on
a minor scale. The Shi'is comprise the poorer part of the population.
The ruling family and most wealthy merchants are Sunni. Five out of
seventeen ministers are Shi'i, although in the less important ministries.
The Shi'i community is divided between native Shi'is who speak Arabic,
and foreign labourers who happen to be Shi'ites—Iranians, Pakistanis or
Shi'i Iraqis. This is an advantage to the ruling Sunnis, but it can also be
a source of concern because of the danger that a revolutionary attitude
could spread from the native Shi'is to the foreign Shi'is and from them
to all foreign workers. The latter, as in all Gulf oil states, constitute a
somewhat underprivileged class of strangers admitted provisionally and
with limited rights in Bahrain.
    The authorities decided to cut to the root of Shi'i troubles and, in
October 1979, expelled a Shi'i shaikh who called himself the representa-
tive of 'imam' Khomeiny in Bahrain. Since then the Shi'is have been
quiescent. Iraq seized the occasion to emphasize repeatedly that its
army would be at the disposal of Bahrain and any other Arab Gulf state
to defend the Arab nature of the Gulf, but the Bahrainis replied that
such aid was not needed at the present time. It is very doubtful that the

rulers would welcome the thought of Iraqi armed forces landing on their islands, because Iraqi ambitions to play an increased political role in the Gulf are well known, and so far all the Gulf states have collaborated informally but firmly to keep such ambitions in check. If need be, Bahrain would probably first call for Saudi aid. Informal collaboration of the interior ministers and security chiefs between Saudi Arabia, Kuwait, Bahrain and other Gulf states has been established for many years and was reinforced after the Iranian revolution, and again after the latest Shi'i demonstrations.

Kuwait

Kuwait had a constitution and a parliament from 1963 to 1976. There were regular elections, but after each four-year period the size and influence of the opposition increased. Although it remained a minority in the chamber, the influence of the parliament was much greater than was indicated by mere members, in part because it found an important echo among the Palestinians who constitute an important and active minority in Kuwait, notwithstanding the fact that they have no civic rights such as the Kuwaiti citizens enjoy.

Furthermore, the opposition in parliament managed to champion generally popular causes and sometimes obtained the backing of significant section of the pro-government deputies. This was the case in a famous debate in 1972 when the chamber forced the government to nationalize the Kuwait Oil Company in its entirety and not just 75 per cent of it, as the government had proposed.

In private, some of the opposition deputies—perhaps most clearly and convincingly Dr Ahmed al-Khatib (one of the heads of a branch of the pro-Haraka groupings)—posed a whole range of questions relating to the position of privilege enjoyed by the ruling family and, more generally, by all Kuwaiti citizens as compared to Arab immigrants and to foreigners as a whole. According to the Haraka, Arab oil riches ought to profit all Arabs (including the Palestinians and Palestine) and not just a few 'feudal' families and some privileged small groups. They maintained that the Arab states, as they exist today, do not have a right to exist and to act as sovereign states, according to Haraka, because their frontiers are artificial and were imposed by 'colonialism' on an Arab nation which really ought to form one whole. It is easy to see that for anybody holding such beliefs the case of Kuwait, detached from the rest of the Arab territories in 1913 by British colonial action (basically at that time in context of growing German influence immediately before the First World War), and later maintained and consolidated as a 'state' due to its oil riches, represents an especially glaring case of the 'colonialist' *divide et impera* policy applied to the Arab world and which persists thanks to 'feudal' interests implanted and fostered by those same colonialists.

8

Such criticisms struck at the heart of royal rule and called into question the very existence of Kuwait. Citizenship policies are also especially sensitive for many of the same reasons.

The end of the Kuwaiti parliament

On 29 August 1976 parliament in Kuwait was finally suspended for a period of four years. Those parts of the constitution which had guaranteed freedom of the press and postulated new elections after each dissolution of parliament also went into suspension. The reasons for the step were never made quite clear. The press was forbidden to write about them. However, it was hinted officially that the dissolution had something to do with the Palestinians who were said (in presumably inspired press reports outside of Kuwait) to have been in a dangerous mood of despair and radicalism induced by the battles and troubles in Lebanon and then by their culmination. One frequently voiced explanation for the suspension of parliament was that the Palestinians had lost their provisional homes in Lebanon and that it was feared they could try to turn Kuwait into a new provisional home for themselves.

This may have been in part, but it was certainly not the whole truth. It seems most likely that the Palestinians living in Kuwait were blamed because they were close to the opposition (in fact they had amalgamated with it) and at the same time it was easier to attack them than the elected Kuwaiti deputies.

Another part of the truth was that Saudi Arabia had always been unhappy about the establishment of parliaments on the Arabian peninsula. The Kuwaiti parliament, where the most lively debates took place (some of them about such sensitive issues as the privileges of the ruling house) had been the most conspicuous. (Bahrain had by then already abolished its assembly.)

The central issue, however, which led to the dissolution and to the subsequent silencing of the opposition press was almost certainly the clash of wills and of interests which had developed between opposition and government. The government basically consisted of representatives of the ruling family who held all the key positions. It was presided over by the successor to the throne, acting as prime minister. There had been attacks on some of the ministers who belonged to the ruling house on the unwritten law which assured them of key positions. There was a still distant but not impossible danger of the government being brought down by the chamber, as the assembly came more and more under the influence of the opposition groupings. This would have been an intolerable blow to the ruling house. The ruler and his councillors obviously preferred to prevent such developments by ending the parliamentarian experiment quickly.

A revised constitution has been promised for 1980. An assembly of experts is to rewrite it 'in harmony with the spirit of our islamic law and our traditions' and 'in order to safeguard the unity of our homeland its stability and a democratic power', as the dissolution order of 1976 had put it. The new text has not yet been revealed but it will probably contain devices which make it impossible for the chamber to overthrow the government, thus reducing the assembly to a consultative role.

Professional groups closed down

When the Kuwaiti parliament was dissolved in 1976 the professional associations of the Kuwaiti lawyers and journalists were also closed. This happened because they had become the meeting grounds of professionals from Kuwait with those of other Arab countries and, above all, with the Palestinians. These groups short-circuited to some extent the superimposed pyramidal system and helped the circulation of ideas. Such ideas probably subverted the existing order of things. Questioning of the privileges of the Kuwaiti ruling class was justified in the eyes of other Arab groups who were on the whole more qualified than themselves in their professional skills.

In the following year the authorities also closed the Patriotic Club of Kuwait (an-Nadi al-Watani). This had been the most significant meeting ground of the Palestinians and the Kuwaitis who felt inclined towards pan-Arabism (calling itself Arab Nationalism) or towards the Palestinian struggle for their home country which is generally considered a duty incumbent on all Arabs. The closure of this club has been the clearest indication given by the authorities so far that they are watching closely the growing links between the Palestinian minority (close to 25 per cent of the total population of Kuwait) and the Kuwaiti professionals and leaders of the emerging bourgeoisie. The reasons are clear. Any amalgamation between those two influential groups could prove dangerous for the ruling stratum of Kuwaiti shaikhs. They would have the capacity to rule the country and they are open to the basically Palestinian or pan-Arab argument that Kuwait ought to abolish 'feudalism' and place itself at the unconditional service of Arab Nationalism and the Palestine cause, not just by giving aid (which is what the present regime does) but by founding a new regime, basically nationalist oriented (i.e. pan-Arabic) and much more closely allied both to pan-Arab and Palestinian aspirations. When the government acts against the meeting grounds of those two strata of Kuwaiti society it makes clear its awareness of the dangers such interactions can bring for itself and it underlines its will to keep separate from the Kuwaiti citizens what can be classed as 'foreign' Palestinians and other Arabs.

Procedures are much more direct against non-Arab foreigners. According to Kuwait police department records, 18,000 persons were expelled from Kuwait in the last three months of 1979, i.e. between

200 and 250 every day. They were mostly simple people who came as labourers. Some were Iraqis but most were non-Arab and they were expelled because their papers were not in order. However, there are many more whose papers are also not in order but who manage to stay on—partly because they prove useful in their jobs and thus gain the protection of their bosses, Kuwaiti or otherwise, who help them to regularize their situation, and partly because they do not make themsleves conspicuous by political or trade union activities.

The Kuwaiti pyramid

In the meantime a certain amount of stability in Kuwait is induced by the complex and finely graded pyramid of privilege and power on which the state rests. From top to bottom it is structured as follows: ruler, key ministers from the ruling house, other ministers, Kuwaiti citizens, Palestinians, other Arab immigrants and, at the bottom, non-Arab immigrants. The Kuwaiti citizens can be subdivided into native Kuwaitis and other Arabs and foreigners who have been admitted to citizenship. All those ranks correspond to positions of privilege relative to the one immediately below, and it is clear that in the vast majority of cases each rank concentrates on preserving its own privileges and excluding the one underneath from ascending. This makes for enough internal antagonisms, finely differentiated from layer to layer, to ensure security for the leadership.

The case of the Palestinians provides an illustration of the kind of issue involved. For the moderate Palestinian groups, Fatah above all, Kuwait represents a reservoir of money. Important financial contributions to the movement come from the government directly and even more from 'taxes' the PLO is allowed to collect—or even helped by the government to collect—from Palestinians residing in Kuwait. If they were to quarrel with the government the Palestinians would lose those advantages. There are some groups amongst them who would care little, even as the more radical minorities—the Popular Front (Habash) or the Popular Democratic Front (Hawatmeh—but they are kept in check by their own Palestinian majority following Fatah and wanting to avoid what the Palestinians call 'secondary issues' (such as internal fights in the Arab countries outside Palestine). The rulers of Kuwait can thus rely on the Palestinians policing themselves as long as they obtain financial contributions of substance from the country.

For other groups it is similarily the risk of losing their relatively comfortable position which makes them keep their own 'class' and the 'class' below themselves in order. This is even true of the non-Arab immigrant workers who are badly paid and enjoy few of the privileges of social welfare reserved for the Kuwaitis and the immigrant Arabs (at least those who have regular papers, which is not always the case) but who risk expulsion to their homeland where they would be considerably worse off.

Since the owners of privilege in the top ranks of the pyramidal structure do not owe their position to any special skill or efficiency, the whole structure is dependent on oil money permeating it from top to bottom. The top layers, not being especially productive, keep their position by appropriating a relatively large part of that money, either directly via the treasury of the ruler or indirectly via more or less ample sinecures in the state bureaucracies. Even those lower classes who generally work for their money live ultimately on the reminder of the oil royalties since without them there would be very little true productivity. Looking to the still fairly distant future when there will be little oil left, there is an attempt to make Kuwaiti society more productive and less dependent on oil money but it is unlikely that it can be replaced by any other productive activity. Basically, the whole social structure such as it is today has been produced by oil wealth and seems to be dependent on it for its maintenance and inner cohesion, and the top ranks are occupied by essentially non-productive people. However, as long as the oil flows and the wealth trickles down, it will probably remain stable—at least so long as it is not disturbed from the outside.

The decisive question of 'gradation'

The principal characteristic of Kuwaiti pyramid of privilege as compared to that of Saudi Arabia seems to be its fine gradation. This means that the different layers of privilege have preserved some contact with members of the lower half of each level being aware of the danger of dropping down or being engulfed by the stratum below. Each layer, therefore, has a considerable interest in keeping its own group in order, so as to avoid the danger of collapse of the whole, and to keep those below in their place, to avoid losing its own position.

There are no large gaps between the strata as in Saudi Arabia where society tends to split itself more and more into the super-rich able to profit immensely from the oil money and the degraded and proletarianized poor who are victims of inflation, deracination and loss of their traditional ways of life and means of subsistence. The fine gradation in Kuwait is no doubt the fruit of careful policies to raise up the Kuwaiti poor and unskilled (through housing, free building sites, obligatory Kuwaiti participation in foreign businesses, etc.) and to give the immigrants reasonable rewards through salaries, while keeping away undesirables and superfluous foreign elements. Nevertheless, an administration is needed with some skill and Kuwait acquired this early on, thanks to the Palestinian immigrants who have filled the middle ranks of an administration headed by Kuwaitis. Even the size of the small city state has made for transparency in administrative and social affairs and

12

this has helped greatly. Social differences in absolute terms from top to bottom may be as great or nearly as great as they are in Saudi Arabia, but the difference lies in the presence of many middle strata between these extremes which are in close touch with each other and form one coherent whole. Because everybody participates (although quite unequally) it is a structure which retains its cohesion to a considerable degree. Only when the upper strata are completely divorced from the lower ranks is there a danger that they will neglect the needs of the lower ranks.

The Kuwaiti army

The Kuwaiti army today has 10,000 men and is very well armed. In March 1977 the purchase of Russian SAM rockets created something of a sensation. Military expenses between 1973 and 1976 were $ 4,300 million and, by 1978, they had risen by a further $ 1,500 million. The army grew out of the bodyguard of the ruling house. Its officers have been trained by the British, and it has always been commanded by members of the ruling family itself. It has been expanded primarily against the Iraqi threat, a fact well known although little talked about in Kuwait. At various times Iraq has exerted claims either for the complete annexation of Kuwait or for some parts of its territory. The most recent of these claims were in connection with the building of a big Iraqi naval base close to Kuwaiti shores. There have been periodic military invasions and some occupation of Kuwaiti territory. The Kuwaiti army, therefore, primarily has a tripwire function—it is there to fight against any renewed Iraqi danger with sufficient vigour to enable Kuwaiti diplomacy to mobilize support in the other Arab countries and, if need be, in the rest of the world. A mixture of Arab and world support has in the past proved sufficient to moderate Iraqi claims but the Kuwaitis are well aware that such support is much more likely to materialize if Kuwait itself shows signs of resistance.

The fact that the Kuwaiti army has one clearly defined potential enemy is presumably the main reason for the loyalty of the army. There is no evidence of unrest within their ranks or of any anti-government conspiracies. In fact, it would be against all their interests to conspire against the present regime because its breakdown would inevitably mean a new bid for possession by Iraq. Nor would it be to the advantage of the Kuwaiti professional soldiers (most of whom are of Kuwaiti Bedouin stock) to be overrun by the Iraqi army and incorporated into it on conditions much less attractive then those prevailing at present in Kuwait.

Saudi Arabia

Saudi Arabia is clearly differentiated from the two other regimes by the physical size of the country and by the use which the Saudi system makes of religion. The religious connotation has been with the Wahhabis from their beginnings and it is still very much alive. 'The Koran is our constitution' was a favourite maxim of King Faisal. The Wahhabi current in the regime has been reinforced since 1924, the year of the conquest of Mecca, by the assumption of the role of guardian of the sacred places. But for a great many years the fact that the different provinces of Arabia had been united under one dynasty was also an element of inner tension since each province had its own local traditions and dignitaries. Abdul Aziz, who resigned from 1953 to 1964, had to keep all those tendencies in balance; the most serious challenges to his rule came from his own followers, the Wahhabi Eastern Arabs, when they rose against him. The much maligned policy of multiple marriages of the king to women of all sections of the tribes and regions of his vast realm had to be understood in this context.

Even when the oil money started to come in it was many decades before the essential structures of the vast desert empire were changed. In the city states of Bahrain and Kuwait the influence of new wealth was bound to be much more immediate. The real transformation in Saudi Arabia has begun only recently—in the cities during the reigns of Sa'ud Ibn Abdul Aziz (1953—64) and of Faisal (1964—75), and in the desert and in the villages only after the quadrupling of the oil revenues in 1973. This explains the apparent stability so far enjoyed by the regime. Although the city population has been volatile and accessible to such ideas as Arab Nationalism, Ba'athism, Arab Socialism, etc. for quite a long time, the real power basis of the regime has been the Bedouin, or White army, whose task has been to counterbalance the regular army. The latter has been inclined to undertake coups during the last twenty years and apparently remains so inclined. Many of these attempts have been aborted by the Americans and by the different Arab secret services who have infiltrated the army, but it has been the Bedouin army, until recently loyal to the ruling house and the throne, which has been the main protector of the monarchy. It lives on the bounty of the rulers and is commanded directly by some of them.

Immigration started on a large scale with the Yemen war of 1962—67; much later than in Kuwait. It has been Palestinian only in the cities, but Yemeni all over the country for the Yemenis have become the real labour force of Saudi Arabia. Because of the vastness of the country and its many different sections and divisions, a finely gradated pyramid comparable to that of Kuwait has not come into existence. The gaps between the different layers of the society are correspondingly much wider.

14

Because religion has been used much too blatantly as an instrument of power by the ruling classes for many centuries, a force of cohesion is becoming a divisive influence. The religious laws are officially enforced for the ruled but they are increasingly flaunted by the rulers who seem to imagine—quite wrongly—that their subjects are unaware of their drinking and fornicating as long as it is done in the privacy of their mansions. In the last few years a double standard has evolved and it is spreading and deepening. It separates the ruling class, who use their fortunes to avoid strict obedience to the religious laws by travel abroad and seclusion at home, from the people even though they impose strict laws on their subjects and sometimes enforce them by the cruel punishments prescribed by the Islamic code. As one taxi driver in Riyadh put it recently, 'I agree with cutting off the hands of thieves. But in that case the men of the royal family ought to have no hands left!'

Awareness of the existence of this double standard has spread slowly, in part because Faisal in his lifetime kept the worst abuses in check and because he lived an austere life. But the recent jockeying for power and position inside the ruling house, which is destined to go on for some time, has allowed many of the privileged to escape the constraints of strict supervision by their superiors and elders. In the cities two district societies have evolved. The first is a Muslim one and consists of those subjects whose way of life continues to be controlled by strict application of the law. The second is a 'Westernized', hedonistic, materialistic society essentially preoccupied with making money by whatever means and using it for conspicuous consumption. Instead of the cohesion between the different layers of society evident in Kuwait, the chasms in Saudi Arabia are growing wider and deeper. Religion has thus become an element of division in Saudi society rather than a unifying factor.

There is some awareness among the rulers about this development. It is brought home to them by the numerous military conspiracies which are taking place more or less continuously. Details are always kept secret but there is a continuing trickle of news about officers escaping to seek refuge in Iraq, pilots absconding with their aircraft or about units being punished or investigated because of rebellious movements. None of this news can be checked, but it amounts to considerable evidence of disaffection. The rulers have reacted by imposing very strict controls on foreign workers. There are waves of periodic checks and any foreigner caught without documents on his person is expelled.

The impact of development on the native Saudis is creating a more difficult problem. The rulers seem to believe that it would help if they were to settle the Bedouins and to transform them into labourers. Why they should believe this is inexplicable since it could equally well tend to increase instability, but so great is the pressure of new money that the rulers, in their urge to spend it profitably, seem to feel that settlement is a proper thing for the Bedouin to want. Combined with this is the

15

pressure of well-meaning but financially interested foreigners, mainly American and European, who want to sell Saudi Arabia their particular 'development model' because it is the only one they know and it promotes their desire to sell appliances and furnishings.

Plans appear to be in hand to impose general conscription on the Saudi population and thus to form a 'national army'. If this comes about it will probably spell the end of the regime for an army of this kind is likely to overthrow it. That the need for a national army is felt by the rulers can be seen as a sign of their current deep concern caused, among other things, by the downfall of the Shah. But the remedy which they have been persuaded to adopt is likely to carry with it the worst dangers of all.

The mosque occupation

On 4 November 1979 the Great Mosque of Mecca was occupied and held by a group of armed insurrectionists for several weeks. The authorities did what they could to minimize the significance of the event and have attributed the seizure to 'purely religious' fanatics whom they termed 'Khawarij', taking advantage of the double sense of this term which means both a specific religious sect (Kharijiya) and 'people who have left the consensus of the believers'. In reality there can be no doubt that the action represented a mixed religio-sociological and political protest against the regime and its corrupt and impious behaviour (made worse in the eyes of the believers by its lip service to Islam) and as such was typical of traditional Islam. At the same time the old regional tensions between the Hijaz and Najd provinces seem to have played a role. Perhaps also the old opposition of the time of Abdul Nasser (Arabian Peoples Popular Front) played a part as was claimed in Beirut by an old opponent of the regime (and one time head of government in exile), Nasser as Sayyid. Undoubtedly elements of the army and of the National Guard were also involved.

The event was extremely serious. This was shown by the fact that all army and security commanders were dismissed and replaced by new men once the danger was over. Also there has been an incipient political reaction. Prince Fahd has promised a kind of consultative assembly to channel the discontent which obviously abounds in the kingdom but which has no outlet.

In the past there was a physical link between the tribes and the royal house arising from the systematic policy of King Abdul Aziz who married and then divorced the daughters of the tribal heads. They went home with their babies and received alimony for themselves and the princes. No stigma was attached to this, according to the tradition of the Bedouins, and the consequence of the policy was that some member of the royal house and son of the king grew up in each tribe in physical contact with the tribesmen whose natural spokesman he became at court. This system broke down as the princes left their tribes either in the desert or in the slums accumulating around the big cities and became playboys. Yet the archaic system did function well and it has not been replaced by anything else. The princes, the members of the royal house and the businessmen are thus in danger of isolating themselves more and more from the rest of the country and of losing any sense of what is going on in the unprivileged strata of the kingdom. There are attempts to replace the missing connection by secret service activities but Iran has shown the dangers inherent in such a 'security' approach. The ruling class becomes trapped by their own security services into increasing isolation from reality and at the same time they are detested because of the methods used by the 'security' services. Their power has not yet reached that of Savak in Iran but the danger is there and is bound to increase as long as the channels of communication between the rulers and the ruled are blocked.

The regimes compared

Of the three countries considered here, Saudi Arabia is the most unstable. Money has here dissolved order and social cohesion based on the clan. In the city states of Bahrain and Kuwait a more or less stable society has evolved, characterized by comparatively close contact and interaction between the different layers and strata of the society. These societies are unlikely to change violently as long as they are undisturbed from the outside and so long as oil keeps bringing in money—in big streams in the case of Kuwait, in small but vital trickles at Bahrain.

Stability in Saudi Arabia seems much more precarious. The kingdom has been held together essentially by Bedouin loyalties reinforced by a religious bond, and both are being eroded by money. The process of erosion has already gone quite far, and there is probably little that can be done about it at this stage. Liberalization would be fatal, because it will only quicken decay. More and tighter security may help in the short run, but in the long run it will increase the probability of a military coup because the officers and men of the regular and of the Bedouin army are bound to resent the presence and operation of security men in their midst, particularly if they are, as is the case in Saudi Arabia, foreigners or foreign trained. The increased size and technology of the army coupled with renunciation of the principles on which the Bedouin army has built, can only have disastrous consequences for the Saudi regime.

Saudi society will inevitably develop in directions which will foster instability and multiply reasons for resentment, because the country is already split between rich and poor. The ruling class is deeply corrupt and they preach one thing to their subjects and do the opposite. Yet further development means even more money and power for these ruling groups and more corruption. For the subjects it primarily means inflation and alienation. There are no Mullahs in Saudi Arabia independent enough of government supervision and finance to articulate these resentments. This means that it will probably be the army around which opposition elements will coalesce and which will one day liquidate the Saudi regime.

This also in all probability will be the end of stability for the smaller Gulf countries, and it will very probably open up an era of Saudi–Iraqi Arab nationalist and anti-American rivalry and *surenchere*. It is not easy to suggest ways of averting the impending disaster for Saudi society is too opaque for the outsider to perceive anything but the mere outlines. Perhaps the projected consultative assembly is a step in the right direction, but it may already be too late and pressures are such that a loosening of the controls and opening the channels of communication may only accelerate the break up of the regime. It would be advisable to have a small tribally loyal elite army but the rulers seem to be heading towards a policy of general conscription and of dissolving the White or Bedouin army. This is almost certainly a step towards a *coup d'etat*. Generally the political structures are such that there is little chance of reasonable advice from whatever source reaches the rulers. The ruling family itself is at cross purposes and whatever one faction wants to do will probably be checked by the opposite group. This stalemate makes it unlikely that the little time available to counteract the pressures outlined will be used profitably by the Saudi leadership.

2 Transformation amidst tradition: the UAE in transition

John Duke Anthony

The United Arab Emirates—the Middle East's longest and most successful experiment to date in regional political integration—is nearing completion of its first decade of existence. The fact that the seven previously independent shaikhdoms which agreed to form a loose confederation on 2 December 1971 are still together is, by any standard, a remarkable achievement; Only a minority of observers present at the UAE's creation were confident of the fledgling union's ability to survive the first six months, let alone half a decade. Having come this far despite numerous problems, it is appropriate to consider not only the principal forces and factors affecting the union's development since its inception but also, in the face of an uncertain future, its prospects until 1981 when the provisional constitution expires.

Integrative factors

The removal of external threats

At its birth, the UAE was faced with several thorny territorial and external security problems. On the day before the federation came into being, Iran occupied three islands in the Gulf claimed by Ra's al-Khaymah and Sharjah. Moreover, to the south, leftist guerrillas were seeking to topple the dynasty in neighbouring Oman and carry their revolutionary ideology to the Gulf; Iraq was lending support to various dissident groups seeking to unseat the emirates' governments; and a longstanding border dispute between Abu Dhabi and Saudi Arabia prevented the union from establishing diplomatic relations with its most powerful Arab neighbour.

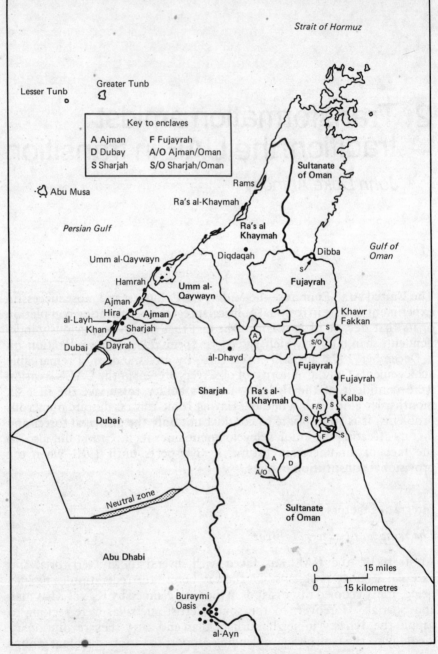

Key to enclaves

A Ajman	F Fujayrah
D Dubay	A/O Ajman/Oman
S Sharjah	S/O Sharjah/Oman

Strait of Hormuz

Lesser Tunb

Greater Tunb

Abu Musa

Persian Gulf

Rams

Ra's al-Khaymah

Sultanate of Oman

Ra's al Khaymah

Umm al-Qaywayn

Diqdaqah

Dibba

Gulf of Oman

Hamrah

Ajman

Hira

Ajman

Umm al-Qaywayn

Fujayrah

al-Layh

Khan

Sharjah

Khawr Fakkan

Dubai

Dayrah

al-Dhayd

Fujayrah

Dubai

Sharjah

Ra's al-Khaymah

Fujayrah

Kalba

F/S

Neutral zone

Sultanate of Oman

Abu Dhabi

0   15 miles

0   15 kilometres

Buraymi Oasis

al-Ayn

Internal frontiers of the United Arab Emirates

By 1976, however, all of these problems had been solved or appeared manageable. Relations between the UAE and its two largest neighbours, Iran and Saudi Arabia, had improved markedly; political contacts and economic ties between Iran and individual UAE states, especially Dubai and Abu Dhabi, had grown considerably; boundary and other disputes between Saudi Arabia and Abu Dhabi were settled in August 1974, leading to the establishment of diplomatic relations; the Dhofar rebellion in neighbouring Oman was officially brought to an end in December 1975; [1] and the cause for concern about Iraqi intentions toward the emirates had also subsided.[2]

There is growing consensus among the elites of the member states that the federation, as it now exists, does not impinge upon their collective interests as much as some had supposed. It is a truism that not all UAE citizens understand fully what their rulers agreed to upon joining the union. Yet in their daily affairs, most of the politically aware citizens are increasingly cognizant of the relatively few powers that were taken from the individual states and accorded the federation. Equally important, most of the rulers and their supporters remain satisfied with the several constitutional provisions that protect the right of each state to administer its domestic affairs—and a significant portion of its external economic affairs—with a minimum of interference from federal authorities.

The rulers of the poorer, non-oil producing states of 'Ajman, Umm al-Qaywayn, Ra's al-Khaymah and Fujayrah remain the most dependent on the existing framework, in as much as it is the principal if not the sole means whereby they have been able to obtain the economic assistance necessary for developing their societies without having to make major concessions of their individual sovereignty. More specifically, these states have for some time been dependent upon Abu Dhabi's aid. An added inducement to their acceptance of the framework was the fact that this was what Abu Dhabi wanted and indeed stipulated as the *sine qua non* for its continued assistance.

---

1 The insurrection never directly affected the emirates. Although the war lasted for ten years, most of the conflict was waged nearly 600 miles away from the UAE in Dhofar, Oman's southernmost province. Only once, in early 1973, when arms caches were discovered in Abu Dhabi and local members of the rebel movement were arrested, was the rebellion ever considered an immediate threat to the union itself.

2 Iraq and the UAE exchanged ambassadors within a year after the union was founded. Following the signing of the Algiers Accord between Iran and Iraq in March 1975, Baghdad ceased its assistance to the rebels fighting in Oman and to Ba'athist cells previously active in the emirates. Subsequently, relations between Iraq and all the Lower Gulf states, including the UAE, improved considerably, reaching their zenith in the wake of the Camp David accords when all of these states endorsed the 'Camp Baghdad Accords' in opposition to the Egyptian-Israeli peace treaty of March 1979. This is not to say, of course, that relations between these states and Iraq thereafter became or are likely to become cordial. Still fresh in the minds of most emirate leaders is the fact that Iraq was the principal stumbling block preventing the signing of a regional security agreement during the Gulf foreign ministers' meeting in Muscat in late November 1976. In addition, along with post-Shah Iran, Iraq continues to be considered a major external security threat by several Gulf states.

21

These poor emirates' choices are in any case limited. Their lack of oil denies them any meaningful prospect of either increasing their political position within the UAE or improving their chances for survival outside the union. There are those in each emirate who believe that an augmented population base might, if coupled with the eventual discovery of petroleum, be parlayed into a more powerful bargaining position within the union. Ra's al-Khaymah and Sharjah are two emirates which have, at times, pursued policies (such as liberal land purchasing schemes for immigrants) in accordance with this assumption. On the other hand, there are those who contend, with somewhat greater persuasiveness in recent years, that increasing population remains questionable due to the fact that it has not yet been proven successful. These people would argue that, for the present, the problems attendant on a swollen population in terms of the stress thereby put on the still somewhat limited infrastructure (i.e. schools, electricity, water, housing, etc.) can be viewed as net liabilities regardless of the security and economic gains accorded to the military elites and development planners. There also remains a consideration that has less to do with political and economic development *per se* than with questions related to ethnicity, religion and nationalism. To wit: with this area priding itself on being adjacent to the epicentre of the Arab and Islamic worlds, there have always been citizens who have argued that the number of people from other non-Arab and/or non-Muslim countries in their midst should be restricted. Those who argue this point retain an attentive audience for their views.

The three wealthiest emirates—Abu Dhabi, Dubai and Sharjah—have from time to time viewed the federation quite differently. Shaikh Zayid, ruler of Abu Dhabi and president of the UAE, has consistently sought more powers for the federal government, which is funded primarily by Abu Dhabi. Shaikh Rashid, ruler of Dubai, has at times expressed somewhat less than wholehearted support for the federation. For several years in succession, Dubai was a source of considerable irritation to UAE officials in Abu Dhabi and elsewhere owing to charges that it did not pay its share of the budget. Dubai's rival, Sharjah, has from the outset been greatly interested in obtaining a larger voice in federal circles not only for reasons of enhancing its overall position in regional affairs, but also out of an abiding concern for the union itself.

For some time now, each of these states, on balance, has seen its interests being met more readily by remaining in, rather than withdrawing from, the UAE. Of added importance, in the sense that it has served to reinforce this view, have been outside pressures. External influences in favour of unity, emanating especially from Saudi Arabia, and also from the USA and Great Britain, have been a consistent factor inducing Dubai and Ra's al-Khaymah—emirates led by two of the most independent minded rulers in all Arabia—to remain in the union. Conversely, no strong outside encouragement for secession has developed.[1]

There also remains a generation gap in political attitudes towards the federation. The older leaders, whose original loyalties grew out of experiences that predated the union and which were heavily rooted in the more narrowly contrived interests of their particular emirate, tribe, or extended family, continue to find it much more difficult to establish federal loyalties than do members of the younger generation. The latter are much more ready and willing to declare openly their belief in its ongoing validity and viability. It is to this second group, comprising nearly half of the citizenry and cutting politically, socially and economically across all segments of the population, including the ruling households and other families and tribes, that most of the positions of prestige and influence in the UAE—and also in many cases those of real power—are increasingly being transferred.

Because of the shortage of qualified personnel, many high positions have traditionally been held by expatriates or by ruling family members, the latter often lacking sufficient technical training. However, with free education for nationals up to university and post-graduate levels having been available for some years, the educational system has been greatly expanded and improved. Thus, in the longer run (and as happens everywhere when old people die), the balance of leadership will shift even more in favour of the younger generation. Even in the relatively short span of less than a decade, the record of achievement in this regard has been impressive. And there is reason to expect that this trend will be accelerated in the near future owing to the likelihood of the aging rulers of 'Ajman and Umm al-Qaywayn, who came to power in 1928 and 1929 respectively, either passing on or yielding to pressures in favour of their abdication.

Integration of the armed forces of the member states

When the UAE was established, each shaikhdom was assured that its own defence establishment could be retained and, if necessary, expanded. As a consequence, the Abu Dhabi Defence Force (ADDF) quickly grew to a size five times greater than the federal Union Defence Force (UDF). This gave cause for concern among the other members and began to fuel internal arms rivalries that might otherwise have been avoided. In May 1976, however, the flags of each of the emirate armies were run down and federal banners hoisted in their place as they became units of a re-unified federal defence force. The creation of a single defence force with

---

1 During the period prior to the overthrow of the Pahlavi dynasty in Iran, however, it was widely believed that Dubai's less than wholehearted support for the union's programmes and policies—and periodic reports that Dubai might consider 'going it alone'—enjoyed the personal endorsement of the Shah.

both internal and external security responsibilities for the UAE as a whole as well as the individual emirates is perhaps the most impressive example to date of the growth of integrative forces within the federation.[1]

Integration of information policies

From the beginning of the federation's existence, union authorities were bedevilled by the persistence of an unco-ordinated network of media outlets and policies among the emirates. The establishment of separate, and often competing, news stations throughout the UAE frequently resulted in the dissemination of knowledge relating to UAE affairs that was either misinformed, inaccurate or, in some cases, in direct opposition to stated union policies. Some of the more embarrassing episodes related to the different positions taken by several of the emirates on foreign oil concessions. For example, during delicate negotiations over Abu Dhabi's acquiring 60 per cent equity participation in its own oil industry, Dubai Radio announced without Abu Dhabi's prior knowledge that Dubai had just successfully achieved 100 per cent equity participation (even if it was more a 'paper' 100 per cent than a real one) in Dubai Petroleum Company.

This kind of lack of co-operation has been reduced since 1976, when co-ordination of the media was placed under a federal broadcasting agency. The morale of federal spokesmen subsequently rose noticeably as opportunities for individual emirates to use the media to undermine union-wide policies were thereby decreased considerably. This development received an unexpected impetus in mid 1979 when the ruler of Dubai, who along with his counterpart in Ra's al-Khaymah had frequently pursued policies in his own emirate that were at odds with UAE goals, agreed to become the federation's prime minister.

Diminishing dependence on expatriates in key sectors

The primary force that first brought the emirates together and kept them united was the expatriate, largely British, presence. This group was also the backbone of local administrations in many of the emirates. There were less than forty UAE citizens with university degrees at the time—not a single lawyer or judge, and probably no more than a dozen individuals among the indigenous inhabitants with advanced training in petroleum economics, financial management or development planning.

1 Control of the military command structure, as opposed to the integration of its constituent units, however, has been a more controversial issue. The matter occasioned a minor political crisis when Shaikh Zayid appointed his second eldest son, Sandhurst trained Shaikh Sultan, as Commander of the UAE Defence Force in 1978. Shaikh Muhammad, third son of the ruler of Dubai (and UAE Vice-President) Shaikh Rashid, however, has held the important post of Minister of Defence since the UAE's inception.

In order to get the federation to work, therefore, it was necessary to retain or place skilled expatriates at all levels of the administrative, economic and defence structures. Fortunately for the union, the sizeable body of foreign specialists already present was willing to remain, permitting a much smoother transition to independence than might otherwise have been possible.

The day is fast approaching, however, when UAE citizens, with the help of foreign Arabs, will be able to take over completely from the non-Arab expatriates and administer the federation by themselves. Native expertise has been and continues to be demonstrated with impressive frequency in many fields. Oil, finance and foreign affairs remain in the forefront as the UAE has repeatedly provided evidence of an ability to act with independence of mind and purpose in regional matters affecting the wider Arab and Islamic worlds. The union's stand with Saudi Arabia in December 1976 against the rest of OPEC on the issue of oil prices is perhaps the best known case in point. Some observers give greater credit for this development to the self-assurance of Shaikh Zayid and the great improvement in Saudi—Abu Dhabi relations. Even so, no one since has gainsayed the thesis that it was also the product of a growing spirit of confidence within the UAE government itself.

In sum, evidence of a diverse and diffuse nature continues to mount which would indicate that favourable attitudes toward continuing the federation for the foreseeable future have indeed taken root throughout the UAE. In assessing that future, however, these signs of progress must be weighed against a number of shortcomings which, all along, have sapped the union's vitality and which could, unless somehow checked, easily undermine the logic of its unity, both now and in the future.

Disintegrative forces

The perpetuation of rivalries and jealousies

No one expected that these seven previously separate shaikhdoms would, upon joining the union, bury overnight their longstanding rivalries. Indeed, one reason why it took more than three years to establish the UAE was the deeply embedded tensions existing among them.

The better part of a decade is by no means to be construed as an insignificant span of time. Yet in this case it has been too limited a period to allay the suspicions and distrusts of a century. In recent years, moreover, the discovery of oil has served as much to exacerbate as to ameliorate intra-UAE rivalries. Recognizing their inability to stand alone without an adequate economic base, every ruling house in the UAE has been and to this day remains titillated with dreams of grandeur by the existence or possibility of the discovery of oil. None of them, however, has a chance to fulfill such hopes without oil, and none of those who have it can benefit so well if their respective sovereignties are submerged in the federation.

The calibre of UAE government personnel

When the federal experiment began, many senior policy positions were awarded to members of the various ruling families and others with little or no regard for their qualifications. Competition for such jobs was fierce. Moreover, the difficulty was compounded by the necessity of maintaining at least a semblance of balance in positions among the emirates, the smaller of which have until recently had very few university graduates available. This shortcoming was mitigated by the appointment of deputy ministers and permanent secretaries who were selected more on the basis of merit. Even so, the ministers themselves retained ultimate decision making authority. Thus, despite sound advice by expatriates and a growing number of qualified local bureaucrats, there have been numerous cases of incompetence, particularly in approving unsound projects. The problem has at times been exacerbated as expatriates and local citizens have attempted to promote the interests of individual contracting and consulting firms.

Moreover, even as an increasing number of citizens return from abroad with a higher education, the services of many who might otherwise opt for a UAE government career are more often than not recruited instead by the private sector, owing to the more lucrative opportunities to be had in business, or, as has happened in some instances, by the local government of their native emirate. This internal 'brain drain', should it persist, will continue to retard the development and efficiency of federal government institutions for some time to come.[1]

Unresolved border disputes

The political map of the union demonstrates graphically the complexity of boundary arrangements among the UAE member states. All but Abu Dhabi and Umm al-Qaywayn lay claim to sovereignty over non-contiguous territories, generally determined by tribal affiliation. As a result, the existence of numerous border disputes has long been a barrier to co-operation among the member states of the UAE. Although oil exploration provided a catalyst for settling some two dozen contested areas in the 1950s, close to a dozen disputes remain.

---

1 Even at the time of writing, nearly every single professional, technical and managerial position in the UAE in such administratively, militarily and economically critical areas of endeavour as utilities and communications is still staffed by foreigners.

Even some of the 'settled' disputes, however, still rankle. For example, the offshore boundary dispute between Umm al-Qaywayn and Sharjah was settled in a formula whereby Sharjah pays Umm al-Qaywayn a percentage of the revenues from oil produced in the area formerly claimed by the latter, but only after total revenues from production have been first shared with Iran. Having, in effect, to stand third in line remains as humiliating for the people of Umm al-Qaywayn in 1979 as it was in 1971 when they lost control of the area to Sharjah in the first place. Moreover, declining production in the Abu Musa field means that Umm al-Qaywayn's income from this source will also decline unless Sharjah agrees to a new sharing formula.

A territorial dispute on the UAE's east coast developed in May 1972 when Fujayran and Sharjan tribesmen fought a violent series of battles in which two dozen died. The presence there of UAE military units has been required ever since. A third boundary conflict, between Dubai and Sharjah, was one reason why Shaikh Zayid threatened in August 1976 not to run for re-election as president of the UAE for another five year term. This boundary dispute is complicated further by the fact that important economic issues have been involved. The land in contention was to have been the site of Sharjah's Charles de Gaulle Financial Centre, which the commercial elites of neighbouring Dubai perceived as a bid by their counterparts in Sharjah to lure away business firms that were already located in, or were contemplating moving to, Dubai.

The question of succession in key states

The question of rulership succession in the UAE states has historically been surrounded by intrigue and, on occasion, murder. This persisted even during the period of British protection. In the past, the absence of a clearly agreed upon successor has provided fertile ground for dynastic intrigue among relatives of the various rulers and, on more than one occasion, has resulted in the premature removal of a ruler from power. It is still too early to tell, however, how much the creation of the federation will mitigate this violent and stormy tradition, particularly in view of the fact that the individuals who would fill the post of heir apparent have not yet been selected in several UAE states.

The impact of geography and changing technology on the economic fortunes of key UAE states

For many years Abu Dhabi and Sharjah have been intensely jealous of neighbouring Dubai. Abu Dhabi's jealousy of Dubai's phenomenal commercial success has been reinforced by its ongoing dependence on Dubai's merchants for a substantial portion of its supplies. Some members of the ruling family also still resent the fact that Dubai's success is in part attributable to its having seceded from Abu Dhabi during the last century and that Dubai fought an inconclusive war with Abu Dhabi as recently as 1947. Most of all, Dubai, although much smaller, poorer and militarily weaker than Abu Dhabi, managed not only to achieve a position of *de jure* political parity with Abu Dhabi in the UAE at its founding but also was able to place a more impressive group of spokesmen for its interests into the union government than was Abu Dhabi. All of these jealousies and resentments have tended to strengthen the desire of many in Abu Dhabi to put their emirate ahead of Dubai in practically every field imaginable even, in the view of some extremists, at the price of undermining the still fragile federal framework of which both are key members.

Sharjah, for its part, has had equal if not greater reason to be jealous of Dubai. Until the 1950s, when Dubai became the political centre of the former Trucial States, political pre-eminence belonged to Sharjah owing mainly to its position as headquarters for the British Political Agency and the site of a Royal Air Force base. It was partially because of British irritation at Sharjah's ruler (the same one who was deposed in 1965, only to return and murder his cousin, who succeeded him, in the abortive coup of 1972) that Dubai attained commercial pre-eminence over Sharjah during this period. In addition, the two states were at war with one another as recently as the late 1930s and early 1940s and, unlike Abu Dhabi and Dubai, significant territorial disputes—as noted above—still exist between them. The al-Qasimi rulers of Sharjah and Ra's al-Khaymah have also tended to look down on the al-Maktum dynasty of Dubai. It was therefore doubly galling to Sharjah to take a back seat to Dubai and Abu Dhabi at independence, being denied the right, which the other two have, to veto any proposal put forth in the federation.

Abu Dhabi city, as the capital of the UAE, has already eclipsed Dubai politically. Dubai's commercial pre-eminence could also be undercut, although hardly eclipsed, as the result of two recent developments. The first is the road which lies inward from the shoreline between Abu Dhabi and Qatar that will link the UAE directly to Europe, the source of a substantial proportion of the country's imports. Construction of the road has proceeded slowly over the past five years, but it is expected to be completed some time in 1980.

Since the road will reach Abu Dhabi first, it remains to be seen whether much of the traditional transhipment of goods bound for Abu Dhabi through the port of Dubai will be as necessary as before, and whether, as overland transit from Europe begins to compete with shipping, Abu Dhabi merchants can become more competitive with Dubai merchants than has hitherto been the case.

At the same time, Sharjah has continued to develop port facilities at Khor Fakkan on the Gulf of Oman. Although relatively close by road to the rest of the UAE it is considerably closer by sea from outside the Gulf and, as Lloyds of London took note in 1979, has the added advantage of obviating the need to traverse the heavily sailed Straits of Hormuz, thus lowering insurance rates. The shorter distance would also mean savings on travel time, fuel and personnel costs for shippers.

Khor Fakkan's prospects have increased markedly in the past few years with the ongoing problems of port congestion and shipping delays plaguing many Arabian Peninsula ports. There is also a growing interest among shipping firms in containerization, for which Khor Fakkan, with its ability to handle ships of forty foot draught (i.e. ten feet more than any other port in the UAE) is regarded as the most convenient location for the modern roll-on, roll-off method of discharging cargo. In addition, Sharjah has persisted in its efforts to provide a system of rapid transit of cargo through co-ordinated air and sea port facilities. For these reasons, Sharjah merchants also stand to become more competitive with Dubai's merchants.

None of this need be interpreted as an imminent death knell to Dubai's string of astounding commercial achievements to date. It does, however, underscore the limits regarding the use to which even a highly developed sense of commercial acumen, for which Dubai is renowned, can be put when apolitical geographic and technological forces, over which neither Dubai nor anyone else has control, are introduced into the situation. How and whether Dubai will be able to cope with these new developments will deserve close watching. (Should the emirate ultimately prove unable to meet this challenge—unlike any other it has encountered so far—demands from Sharjah for a fundamental realignment of UAE political power would appear almost certain.) Whether Dubai would be willing to acquiesce in such demands or whether, to avoid confrontation, it would move to secure its interests by seceding from the union, is questionable. Equally uncertain is whether Sharjah could or would permit such a realignment to be vetoed or otherwise prohibited by Dubai. The acceptance of the post of UAE premier by Dubai ruler Shaikh Rashid in July 1979 served to some extent to lessen the apprehensions of insiders and outsiders alike as to the first scenario, even though it shed little if any light on the likely outcome of the second one.

The lack of effective industrial co-ordination

Dating from the period prior to the union's establishment, a pattern of ostentatious expenditure has frequently characterized some of the investment and development projects launched by the various emirates. First, various emirates wanted their own 'international' airport, then an 'international' harbour, then cement factories, then container ports, then petro-chemical plants, then skyscraper hotels and, most recently,

29

'international' trade centres. These highly visible, costly and often duplicatory schemes were launched in accordance with decisions made not by federal agencies responsible for development on a regional basis, but by the rulers of the individual emirates. The impetus for these projects continues to be 'one-upmanship' and inter-emirate competition for commercial pre-eminence and regional prestige. For most of the life of the UAE so far, relatively little thought and even less in the way of serious discussion and debate appears to have been given as to how the interests of the union as a whole might be affected.

Outsiders, anxious to win lucrative contracts, have consistently taken advantage of these features of competitive one-upmanship among the UAE member states. Numerous foreign consultants, not to mention ambitious local entrepreneurs, have encouraged the various ruling households to believe that they can successfully develop separately from their neighbours and, in certain fields, even from the UAE. Various members of the political elites of Dubai, Ra's al-Khaymah, and to a lesser extent Sharjah, have consistently entertained ambitions of independent statehood or relative autonomy within the UAE. For this reason alone, the continued existence of the UAE remains uncertain.

Intra-UAE competition has been persistent. As a consequence, there is reason to wonder whether a union of the emirates, however loosely organized, might be expected to survive and, if so, for how long. The question mark remains so long as individual rulers are permitted to pursue unchecked the more parochial interests of their respective emirates, regardless of whether these serve federal interests. The failure to date of federal ministries to act as a screening, checking—and, where necessary, blocking—device on projects of a 'showpiece' nature has permitted a number of ill-planned expenditures on programmes that have had a negative effect on the UAE's regional and international image. (Unfortunately for the cause of federation in the UAE, the fact that the union ministries lack both legal and practical authority, as well as funds, to control most of these projects, would seem to indicate that this situation is likely to continue for some time to come.)

Immigration

Immigration as an issue pertinent to federal and emirate development goals continues to be a subject of widespread discussion and debate throughout the UAE. In terms of its political and socio-economic implications, it remains one of the two or three most important questions confronting union decision makers. While British officials involved with development planning were mindful of the issue as early as the mid 1960s, public admission of serious concern in the highest echelons of UAE officialdom dates mainly from the formation of a revised

Council of Ministers in 1977. Since then the youngest ministers—most of whom enjoy support on immigration matters from a wide strata of the citizenry—have kept the issue at the forefront. Their concerns, all of which are shared by the older generation, are rooted in a tangled web that links such questions as ethnicity, social change, and internal security to the federation's prospects for economic wellbeing and long term political stability.

An early sign of progress in coming to grips with the matter was the publication, even before the 1977 cabinet came into being, of a Ministry of Labour and Social Affairs requirement for all aliens without valid work permits to come forth and register or re-register as foreign workers. A period of grace was proclaimed from August to November 1976, during which time an amnesty would apply to all those whose documents contained irregularities. The most astonishing result was that some 100,000 foreigners took advantage of the offer. In so doing, they tacitly acknowledged that their presence in the UAE had been 'illegal'.

In the process of obtaining such data, however, the problem became not only one of imposing order and efficiency on a previously near chaotic situation. It also reflected a larger, much more pervasive concern of a philosophical nature, and served to raise a wide variety of human-istic questions for which conventional wisdom offers no easy answers. Moving the immigration issue to centre stage, in short, has revealed an immense amount of societal anxiety about how UAE citizens should go about confronting the outside world and the future.

The basis for UAE officialdom's concern remains unassailable. The children of senior government officials are a distinct minority in class-rooms averaging 55 students. These officials view a situation in which the overwhelming majority of the pupils are foreigners as one that warrants their legitimate concern. Their fear is that their children will not be inculcated with a sufficient sense of 'UAE-ness' in the course of their education.

The immigration problem in the classroom is different from the one at the working class level. The latter, an almost exclusively adult male phenomenon, can be viewed daily and most dramatically among the thousands of aliens engaged in port or construction work or among those, from Oman and elsewhere, who bear the union's weaponry—but not its passport. In its cultural and civilizational context, the educational dimension of the difficulty is twofold. First, the local students are taught not by their fellow citizens but by Egyptians, Jordanians, Palestinians, Indians and Pakistanis. These and other expatriate teachers have little knowledge or appreciation of the indigenous culture of the UAE area. Worse, on such occasions when some of them deign to speak of the country as a whole or its governmental establishment in particular, it is often in patronizing or negative terms.

Secondly, the immigration problem manifests itself in terms of the

31

nature and orientation of the local student's peer groups. The latter, who in every instance are mainly foreigners, have become an important source of much that a UAE student is learning nowadays in terms of attitudes, behaviour and values. The effect on large numbers of UAE youth of being awash, as it were, in a sea of aliens has been to leave them confused and disoriented as to the ultimate source of administration and authority in their country. More troubling, in terms of educational and economic efficiency, it has contributed to the blurred view of many as to the locus of control over some of the union's most basic institutions.

Other UAE citizens are concerned about the immigration issue not only from the perspective of the classroom or the corps of construction workers or foreign mercenaries but equally from that of the enormous costs which the immigration issue entails by the provision of a growing range of health and other social services to the UAE population as a whole. With three-quarters of the nearly 800,000 inhabitants being foreigners, the costs of what some analysts estimate to be 80 per cent of the health facilities allocated to their use represents an inordinately high proportion of the sums involved. Some officials are increasingly finding that such expenditures, whether in absolute or relative terms, are difficult to justify. Their frame of reference is the growing feeling among the citizenry—admittedly based more on emotions and ethnicity than economics—that the majority of the beneficiaries are foreigners who contributed little, if anything, to the expenditures which brought such facilities and services into existence.

What is rapidly emerging from the discussions and debates surrounding the immigration issue, in short, is a rather pronounced 'we—they' consciousness. Such sentiments are particularly noticeable among the politically aware members of the citizenry in Abu Dhabi, Dubai and the other emirates. Neither the phenomenon itself nor its causes, however, are new to the Gulf. What is occurring on an increasingly broad scale in the emirates is nothing less than that which has existed in Kuwait for quite some time: namely a chauvinistic all of 'the UAE for the UAE-ans only'. And, as happened earlier in Kuwait, the issue has increasingly begun to affect the political dynamics of the federal government. If nothing else, the proponents within UAE officialdom of tighter restrictions on the immigrant community are being strengthened daily by the growing incidence of crimes of violence committed by foreigners, not to mention the continuing controversy to which the latter also contribute by virtue of their considerably different lifestyles and values.

As has been the case for much of the past decade, and reflective of a nearly identical situation in this regard in Kuwait, Qatar, Bahrain and Oman, the great majority of the foreign labour force continues to be engaged in the construction sector of the local economies. Abu Dhabi,

Dubai and Sharjah are most affected. Most if not all of these workers are expected to and actually do return to their native countries when the project for which their services were contracted is completed. Once the basic infrastructural boom is over, it is anticipated that this hitherto almost amorphous sea of aliens will have departed for other lands.

What is especially troubling to federal and emirate decision makers, however, has little to do with this group of immigrant workers. On the contrary, their presence, although never uncontroversial, has been acknowledged by most groups throughout the history of the UAE as having been indispensable to such economic development as has occurred or is being considered. Their concern, rather, is mainly for the kind of permanent foreign labour force that, of necessity, will need to be imported to Dubai, Abu Dhabi and elsewhere in the UAE to run the aluminium smelter, gas liquefaction plants and other industrial ventures already under way or being contemplated. Unlike the first group, this latter element is conservatively estimated to number in the high tens of thousands. The industrial units, in short, will require a stable labour force, even more schools and health facilities than have already been built, plus housing and, eventually, permission and provision for their families to join them, all of which are certain to spell continued stress on an already strained social system as the UAE persists in its efforts to modernize in the fastest possible time.

A related concern is the lack to date of a comprehensive labour law covering the UAE as a whole or, failing that, one which would up-date and give weight to the sole existing labour laws (Dubai, 1965 and Abu Dhabi, 1966). Neither of the latter pieces of legislation is enforceable in practice due to the absence of a corps of trained inspectors in the Ministry of Labour. Adequate legislation or a greater corpus of federal regulation than presently exists is needed not only to facilitate a more co-ordinated approach to the entire range of labour questions on a union-wide basis, but also to contribute to the goal of enhancing internal security. The assassination of Seif Ghobash in the autumn of 1977, the universally revered and exceptionally gifted Minister of State for Foreign Affairs, occasioned great public anguish over a situation—the regulation of foreign labour—which had clearly become out of hand.[1]

The immigration issue also lies at the heart of what is one of the most basic of all developmental questions posed for the union: namely, the kinds of skills that will be needed if Abu Dhabi, Dubai and the other emirates—and indeed, the UAE as a whole—are not only to survive but

---

1 Within UAE officialdom, no one seemed to know anything at all about the background or whereabouts of the assassin until the moment he was apprehended, even though in the course of his interrogation it was revealed that he had been living and working in Abu Dhabi uninterruptedly for five months prior to the event. Throughout that period of time the individual, a Palestinian, had been working as a low level painter while waiting for instructions from abroad on when to kill 'Abd al-Halim al-Kaddam (the Syrian Foreign Minister) for whom the shots were intended but missed.

33

prosper and flourish in the process. In Abu Dhabi, the situation is especially acute and can perhaps be illustrated most dramatically in terms of the military, the ranks of which are filled mostly by foreigners. Indeed, 85 per cent of rank and file are Omani, the remainder being mainly Arab, including local UAE citizens, some Jordanians, plus a considerable number of Baluchis. At the officer level most are UAE citizens, some of whom are naturalized having previously held Jordanian citizenship. There are still a few British military personnel who are retained informally in more or less ex-officio advisory capacities, although none are in uniform or associated with those in command positions.

The task of finding and retaining local citizens already in the military for the purpose of sending them to be trained abroad is more difficult than one might imagine. The problem is to get such individuals out of the country and embarked on their foreign training courses before they resign and succumb to the lucrative inducements pressed on them by relatives and others who persuade them to go into business. The difficulty of instilling and maintaining military discipline in the armed forces—by traditional standards as honourable as any other profession—thus continues to elude an early or easy resolution. An unintended consequence of parallel significance is that, for the same reasons, there is even less hope of instilling and maintaining discipline in a local working class that would be expected in the course of performing whatever manual, casual or other labour required, to serve the industrial sector or the professions.

The problem has emerged in large measure out of the boom which continues to characterize much of contemporary Abu Dhabi, Dubai and most of the other emirates. For many citizens, in short, there seems little reason why they should choose a career as an industrial worker, a soldier or as a member of one of the white collar professions when they can go into business and make, if not a billion dollars, then in any case a great many dirhams. The number of local inhabitants in the military and the professions who have already left and are contemplating leaving their jobs to enter the business sector is alarming. Yet the trend appears certain to continue. That is, the pattern depicted here seems bound to persist so long as the situation remains one in which most, if not all, of the socially repugnant or physically arduous work performed in the UAE is carried out not by the local citizenry but by members of a foreign servant class.

Conclusion

In conclusion, it is clear that the UAE's chances for long run success, and indeed even its prospects for the next few years, are mixed. Despite

34

a growing cohesiveness within the union as a whole, there are many factors—conflicting federal, national, parochial, tribal and dynastic sentiments and competing economic development programmes—that are and will remain beyond the capacity of the union government, as currently structured, to control. Even so, that the seven rulers have elected for the time being to remain in rather than withdraw from the union is evidence enough that the UAE's strengths exceed its weaknesses so far. To be sure, the exact nature of the concessions for strengthening federal authority that the rulers made to Shaikh Zayid during the last half of 1976 is unknown. Moreover, equally unknown is what private agreements may have been negotiated when Shaikh Rashid agreed to become the federation's prime minister. What is most significant would appear to be the fact that Zayid was persuaded to serve for another five year term as UAE president and that Rashid agreed for the first time to accept a degree of personal responsibility for the administration of federal affairs on a day to day basis.

In terms of the most important period ahead—i.e. the period until 1981 which coincides with the second terms of office of both Shaikh Zayid as UAE president and Shaikh Rashid as vice-president and with the extended life of the provisional constitution—it would seem that the UAE stands a good chance of surviving for at least two more years. The union's prospects beyond that point are understandably much more difficult to predict. What seems certain, however, is that many of the issues discussed in this paper that have negatively affected the UAE's prospects to date are likely to have come to a head by then.

Some of the more disquieting issues that will need to be resolved if the UAE is to continue beyond that point are those relating to the formal and actual distribution of authority within the union—issues that are intricately linked to a continuing debate over the federal constitution. The 1976 decision, following months of debate, to extend the life of the provisional constitution, merely postponed a number of fights over the issues of union powers versus emirate powers as these relate to such problems as economic co-ordination and integration and other issues discussed here. These can be expected to surface again, if not in the near future then certainly by 1981 when the provisional constitution must once more be extended or replaced and a new UAE president and vice-president elected.

A matter of concern in this regard is the potential for the constitutional issue itself to become the focus of all the rivalries, tensions and mutual distrust that threaten the continued cohesiveness of the UAE. For example, failure to adopt a permanent constitution or to adopt one giving the UAE greater executive powers might lead Shaikh Zayid to resign as president or even pull Abu Dhabi (and perhaps 'Ajman, Fujayrah and Umm al-Qaywayn along with it) out of the UAE. Conversely, a constitution that strengthened the central government at the emirates' expense or gave Sharjah equality with Dubai might lead Shaikh Rashid to pull Dubai out of the union.[1]

In short, the acid test of whether the other rulers are prepared to accommodate Shaikh Zayid over the long run—and, if so, to what extent and, also quite possibly, on what terms—is still to come. To be sure, a truer indication than verbal commitments to this effect will be the degree to which the other rulers do in fact permit central authority to become commensurate with central responsibility. In this regard, Abu Dhabi, Sharjah, 'Ajman, Umm al-Qaywayn and Fujayrah, for the time being at least, will not prove stumbling blocks.

Before Shaikh Rashid became prime minister, conventional wisdom used to hold that the likely course of action in Dubai and Ra's al-Khaymah would be far less certain. In those two states, barring a change in the leadership or a turnabout in the attitudes of their respective rulers, pundits used to say that the continued prevalence of parochial sentiments and policies at the expense of federalist goals seemed probable. Yet Rashid's acceptance of an appointment to the premiership stunned most analysts. In itself, that act raised as much confusion as certainty in the minds of those who ponder the meaning of its ultimate significance.

Most observers—UAE citizens and outsiders alike—have little difficulty identifying with the determination of the rulers of Dubai and Ra's al-Khaymah to develop their societies as rapidly as possible. Nearly everyone is impressed by the remarkable degree of achievement which Dubai, in particular, has registered in this regard. Equally, many if not all of these same observers view positively the integrative aspirations of the federal apparatus in Abu Dhabi.

Yet a continuing dilemma in the UAE emerges from a basic incompatibility here. It stems from what, in essence, are two very different—some would say contradictory—courses of development. It is not so much, if at all, a matter of saying that both cannot prevail, that one must yield to the other. More accurate perhaps would be the view that there is room for existence between the two extremes: an in-between (not necessarily to be equated with middle) ground between the continued existence of seven independent emirates surviving in what in some fields could become an increasingly strong federation.

1   A set of scenarios in which disintegrative forces existing more in one emirate than in the rest, might affect the union as a whole, would include: a possible situation in which Sharjah, failing to obtain veto powers in the Supreme Council of Rulers, might seek to withdraw from the union; a possible growth of 'Abu Dhabi First' sentiment in the UAE capital, which might foster a move by leading segments in that emirate to withdraw from the union; or a situation in Dubai whereby the merchant community, in reaction to the federal machinery in Abu Dhabi, might press Shaikh Rashid to secede.

At the time of the UAE's founding this problem was not so much solved as pushed aside. Yet more than any other difficulty, it was this that returned repeatedly throughout the first eight years to haunt and hamper the federation's efforts to achieve success. Lacking an early resolution, it will continue to pose immense—in some cases insurmountable—difficulties for emirate and federal leaders in the period ahead. The situation, in short, remains one of a majority of the emirates being willing to permit the federation to play a dominant role, versus some that clearly are interested in exposing whatever other alternatives might exist[1] of seven rulers unable as yet to determine as a group whether, as they proceed with the task of developing their societies, the union—whether as pre-eminent power, helpful collaborator or unwelcomed irritant—is to be in front of, alongside or behind them. Only on a more satisfactory resolution of this question in favour of the federalists than has occurred to date—and not before such a resolution—will the UAE's chances for long run survival be enhanced.

1 Alternative approaches to confronting the future that have been mooted from time to time have usually postulated the creation of a unitary state at such time in the future when a significant portion of the population would come to take the view that the federal structure was no longer viable. Such a hypothesis has usually positioned Abu Dhabi town at the political, administrative and economic centre of any new edifice. Beyond the geographic confines of the federal union, the possibilities become at once more numerous and ingenious. Among the various proposals discussed over the years have been: a 'greater Oman', which would entail a fusing of one or more of the present UAE states with the Sultanate; a revival of the original nine state federation idea for which Bahrain and Qatar were candidates for membership during the 1968—71 period prior to the British withdrawal; the establishment of an interlocking network of relationships just short of a federal apparatus between Kuwait and Bahrain; and a virtual plethora of functional co-operative relationships among all the states of the area, e.g. customs unions, currency standardization, homogenization of health services delivery systems, uniform weights and measures, postal systems, passports, educational curricula, shipping, refining, regional security, etc.

3 Economic problems of Arabian Peninsula oil states

Michael Field

Introduction: a diminishing asset

Every one of the Arabian oil states is deeply concerned with the knowledge that oil is a diminishing resource. They are equally aware that oil is more or less the only natural resource they have. Together, these thoughts have led to an intense preoccupation with the value of oil reserves, with extracting the highest possible price for them and conserving them for as long as possible. It is standard producer rhetoric—particularly in Kuwait where the art has reached its most sophisticated form—to talk of managing the national asset as 'a trust for the generations yet unborn'. These feelings are matched by an equally obsessive concern with oil income accounting for nearly all of the Arabian governments' revenues and all but a fraction of the countries' foreign exchange receipts.

It goes without saying that the first and biggest economic problem for the producers must be the question of how long the oil will last, or more precisely how long it will be before their oil income drops below the level of their spending. This question underlies the first tentative moves being made towards levying domestic taxes, which most Arabians would now regard as an unjust intrustion on their fundamental rights. It underlies the new idea of disabusing citizens of their view of the state as a source of perpetual enrichment, this being a theme occasionally taken up by Abdel-Rahman Atiqi, the Finance Minister of Kuwait. It also dictates the pace at which industrialization programmes are being pushed ahead in the different states. It is certainly seen as being the vital factor in the region's future internal stability.

To date, the massive chanelling of wealth into private hands has been a major force for social contentment in the Gulf—any state would be content if 70 per cent of its nationals had their own private incomes from rents, as is the case in Kuwait. There must be a question of whether this stability will continue if and when the injections of wealth have to stop. At present it is impossible to imagine a more destabilizing problem than the oil producing governments finding themselves running out of money. On the other hand, while the money lasts the Arabian Peninsula oil producers are free of most of the classic afflictions of other developing countries. This is not to say that the producers do not suffer from some of the usual anxieties of reliance on a single resource, or that they have not experienced bottlenecks or high rates of inflation in their efforts to develop fast, or that there are no problems in having very small populations who are unwilling to take up the technical professions or do manual labour. But it does mean that the producers have no balance of payments or budgetary problems, that failures of early diversification projects do not matter in fiscal or export terms, and that the states can buy themselves out of many of their social problems.

To try to suggest dates when the oil producers might find their oil incomes insufficient for their spending would be a fruitless exercise. It would involve too many diverse factors, such as the level of economic growth in the Western economies, and it would have to incorporate a whole range of different 'bases' embracing a time span of up to half a century. Furthermore, it would be irrelevant because there will not be particular dates when individual producers will slide into deficit once and for all. Rather than thinking in terms of this simple 'dividing line' pattern, it would be better to think of a graph in which the two lines representing income and spending draw gradually closer together and then begin continually crossing over each other. As a result of oil price rises the income line will move above the spending line, then as spending rises and production falls (it is already falling in Bahrain and Oman and on the point of falling in Qatar) the income line will dip below the spending line until such time as a crisis in a producer state, a surge in demand in the consumer countries or the drop in supply itself leads to another price rise. The first signs of this pattern have already been visible in the last two or three years: in exceptional circumstances in 1978 even Saudi Arabia ran a small deficit, although now there seems little prospect of the deficit reappearing for a year or two.

The mixed pattern of surpluses and deficits will probably run on until the end of this century or longer. With regard to the income side of their accounts, the producers seem increasingly determined to spin out their reserves for as long as possible, and whatever this may mean for the Western economies it will certainly be beneficial for their own security. The three producers with spare capacity, Saudi Arabia, Kuwait and Abu Dhabi, have all set official ceilings on their output. Kuwait has indeed cut its output to a point where in 1978 it achieved a reserves-production ratio of 97 years. Barring breakthroughs in the development of alternative sources of energy, it also seems fair to assume that as Middle Eastern production falls, for geological or policy reasons, the drop in volume will be more than offset by rises in price. This at least should be the pattern in the early years. On such occasions as income does fall temporarily below spending, the producers will be able to draw on their considerable financial reserves.

On the spending side it is clear that the producers now seem concerned to moderate their expenditure in order to avoid the disruptive social consequences of high inflation and boom-bust cycles. In this context it might be wise in future for the consumers to acquiesce in bigger petrodollar surpluses and put less emphasis on encouraging the producers to spend their revenues. There is no doubt that Western encouragement was partly to blame for the massive spending plans of the Shah of Iran and his deluded opinion that his country could be transformed into a major industrial power by the end of this century.

On the other hand, nobody should persuade himself that now that the producers have embarked upon programmes of massive development it will be possible to cut spending permanently once the initial capital expenditure has been completed. There obviously will be a fall in spending for a time; this can be seen in the consistent surpluses returned by Kuwait, which had installed much of its infrastructure and industry before the 1973—74 oil price rises. However, in the longer term, the current budget will tend to increase with an expanding population and the necessity of staffing and maintaining an ever larger number of social amenities, hospitals, ports, roads, airports and schools. As with amenities anywhere else in the world, the older structures become the higher will be the cost of maintaining them, and in the Arabian Peninsula the harsh climate ages buildings and machinery much faster than in most of the industrialized world.

In spite of this last proviso, the overall prospects for the Arabian oil producers continuing to receive an adequate supply of revenues for a generation seem quite good. Some states are better placed than others. Saudi Arabia, Kuwait and Abu Dhabi are the most secure. Bahrain, Oman and Qatar are in less happy positions, but all are relatively small consumers of revenues and they can rely on receiving help from the others, especially Saudi Arabia. Indeed, Bahrain and Oman are already receiving large amounts of direct and indirect Saudi aid, although they have found it does not come entirely without social and political strings. The important point is that the adequacy of the incomes of these 'poorer' states will be determined not so much by their own oil production as by the production of Saudi Arabia.

Diversification

The development priority of all the oil producers has been infrastructure—roads, ports, airports, telecommunications, seawater desalina-
tion, electric power and sewerage. By the time of the oil price explosion
of 1973—74, these projects were more or less complete in Kuwait and
Bahrain, although they have had to be expanded since, and now, in mid
1980, the infrastructural work is nearly complete in Qatar, Abu Dhabi
and Dubai. It is only in the northern emirates, Oman and Saudi Arabia,
because of their vast size and much bigger populations, that there are
significant numbers of infrastructural contracts still to be awarded.

After infrastructure has come diversification. The producers' awareness of the diminishing nature of their asset has meant that after an
early flush of wild spending, all governments have conceived the major
long term economic ambition of developing supplementary sources of
income. Typically, the pattern has been for major diversification projects
to be started about 15—20 years after the beginning of oil production—
the intervening years having been marked partly by social and infrastructural spending and partly by sheer waste. It was in the first half of
the 1960s that Saudi Arabia and Kuwait planned their original heavy
industries, after beginning significant oil production in both cases in
1946.

The decision to diversify was almost inevitable. The most obvious
alternative—building a massive portfolio of foreign investments—provides a politically insecure souce of income, as Iran's recent experience
with its US assets has shown, and seems not to be acceptable to the
countries that would receive the investments. To be safe from inflation
as well as providing a source of income, a large proportion of the foreign
holdings would have to be in real estate and direct investments in
industry, agriculture or large blocks of shares in major companies. So far
there has been no evidence that the recipient countries would be prepared
to make these investments available to the producers on anything like
the scale that would be required if the producers were eventually to live
off them. Taken as a group, the producers' present investments are
mostly in paper assets, although the smaller investors—Kuwait, Abu
Dhabi and Qatar—do have a large part of their reserves in more substantial forms of holdings. (For the reasons already mentioned, it is probably
only these smaller investors that have the option of trying to put a
significant part of their funds into direct investments. The West will
tolerate receiving in direct investments a fair part of a $40—50 billion
portfolio, which is what Kuwait, Abu Dhabi and Qatar own between
them, but it might not tolerate having a similar proportion of assets
invested direct from a $110—120 billion portfolio, which is the total of
Arabian oil producer governments' foreign holdings if Saudi Arabia is
added in.) In almost all cases—Kuwait being the partial exception—

foreign investments are seen as a means of making up periodic shortfalls of revenue and at a later stage as a supplement to new sources of domestic income: not as the major source of income on which the states will rely when their oil revenues decline.

Another option for the producers would be conservation, which in a sense only postpones the evil day when oil revenues will be inadequate for spending, coupled with slower spending at home. These ideas now seem to be being given greater weight in the producers' planning, but they have to be just one aspect in a multi-pronged approach to the future. All of the producers feel that they have to diversify their sources of income at home, notwithstanding the problems of industrial pollution, the social and security costs of importing large numbers of foreigners, and the dangers of investing in 'white elephants', some of which are inevitable in the early stages of development. (In Arabia the cost of a white elephant is not so much the waste of capital as the labour opportunity cost.) As much as anything else, the producers' decision to diversify is motivated by the pride that comes from self-sufficiency.

Obviously one can count as diversification practically any economic activity that earns new export revenues or saves the import of foreign goods or services and the Arabian Peninsula oil producers have indeed developed a vast range of businesses running from dry docks to irrigated agriculture to an embryonic movie industry. The main emphases, however, seem to have been in heavy process plant industry, light industry, the development of associated and unassociated gas, banking and foreign investment services (mainly in Kuwait and Bahrain) and, in Bahrain, the development of a role as a regional communications, leisure and service centre in which many of the foreign companies operating in the Gulf have established their bases. Dubai, meanwhile, has continued the entrepot trade it built up in the 1950s and 1960s, before its oil came on stream, although the last five years have seen a change in the nature of its business. Whereas it used to be a base for smuggling and legitimate export trade activity, it is now more of a vast shopping emporium in which the bulk of its goods are sold within the state and taken out by the buyers.

The diversification into service industries in Kuwait, Bahrain and Dubai is already an established success—at least in economic terms. There could possibly be problems stemming from Bahrain's role if the indigenous population becomes unhappy with the enormous Western cultural influence that comes from having so many Americans and Europeans on the island, but this is more a political and social issue that lies outside the scope of this paper. As far as Kuwait is concerned, the development of financial institutions has the unqualified advantage of requiring relatively few expatriates and offering careers which Kuwaiti nationals seem to find attractive.

The problems with diversification lie mainly with the development of industry and gas resources, which in revenue supplement terms could make a much bigger contribution than financial services. These industries are examined below.

Heavy industry

The major capital intensive process plants, loosely referred to as 'heavy industries', involve refining, liquified natural gas (frozen mains gas), natural gas liquids (for bottled fuel and chemical feedstocks), petrochemicals, fertilisers, aluminium and steel. Most of these projects are planned to earn export revenues rather than produce import substitutes (the only partial exceptions being steel mills) and all of them have the advantage in the eyes of Middle Eastern planners of making use of the region's abundant resources of 'associated' natural gas (produced with oil), while yielding a large revenue for the size of the labour force employed. The attraction of the projects is increased by the fact that most of the associated gas now produced has to be flared, and would be impracticable to export on a large scale. At present the consumer countries do not have the receiving and distribution facilities to take the gas; the trade in liquified natural gas (LNG) is normally run as a 'service' between a particular liquifaction plant and a particular receiving terminal. Furthermore, given that gas is no more abundant globally than oil, the consumers may prefer to limit the contribution of natural gas to their energy consumption and buy from the Gulf as their present supplies run low in 10 or 15 years time. For the Middle Eastern planners in this case it does not matter if they make gas available to their industries for as little as 20 per cent of the price being paid by the American consumer or 10 per cent of the price received by Algeria for gas exports. There is no opportunity cost in such a pricing policy.

For most of the time that the 'heavy' industrial projects have been under discussion since 1973 they have met with a very sceptical response from economists and journalists in the industrialized world. The main criticisms at the start were that they would encounter operating costs 60–80 per cent above normal Western levels and capital costs of anything from 35–100 per cent above Western levels. There were severe doubts whether these costs could be offset by hidden subsidies in cheap gas, electricity, water and land rental. There were also fears that the severe environment of the Arabian Peninsula, with extreme heat, dust, humidity and saline water supplies, would cause breakdowns leading to long periods of closure and financial losses. Worse still were the marketing prospects. The natural gas liquids (NGL) facilities under construction in Saudi Arabia alone are big enough to double the present NGL capacity of the entire free world outside North America, which has made even the Arabian planners themselves admit that their plant is likely to be underutilized. The refineries and petrochemical plants , in contrast, will account for quite minor proportions (2 or 3 per cent) of world capacity in the 1980s even if all those planned are built, but they will be operating in markets already plagued by huge surpluses. In putting forward all these grounds for scepticism, the Western critics of Arabian industrial plans were able to point to the performance of the existing Arabian heavy industries. With the exception of Aluminium Bahrain (ALBA) and the NGL plants and refineries which were originally owned by oil concessionaires and tied in with their own corporate requirements, the performance of the early Arabian industries has been disastrous. Apart from very high running costs, there have been successions of breakdowns (in its first seven years of operations the Saudi fertiliser plant never ran for a full year at more than 55 per cent of capacity), and marketing operations seem to have had more than their share of bad luck, caused by cyclical slumps and exacerbated by the distance of Arabian plants from the main consumers.

In the last 12 to 18 months, however, a somewhat more optimistic climate has surrounded the Arabian industrialization plans. The established plants in the last two or three years have begun to overcome their technical problems, which suggests that although teething troubles in the Middle East may go on for longer than in the Western world, they are not permanent and can be solved by experience and modifications in design. At the same time, as inflation rates have fallen and bottlenecks have disappeared, estimates of additional capital and operating costs in the Middle East have been reduced to plus 25—40 per cent—levels which probably can be offset by supplies of cheap gas.

Another positive development has been the more rigorous approach towards their projects adopted in the last two years by the producers, who seem to have become more determined to see that the projects they build are really the most competitive they can find. Since 1974 there has been an enormous thinning out of numbers of candidate projects, accompanied by a growing awareness of the need to avoid duplication of projects within the region. To assist regional co-ordination, the Arabian industry ministers at a conference in Qatar in 1976 established the Gulf Organization for Industrial Consulting—although it is not yet clear how much authority this body will wield. As with all organizations of its type, much will depend on the forcefulness of the personalities at the top.

The most important change in the outlook for the heavy industries, however, has been in marketing. Since the Iranian revolution and the new oil crisis the prospects for sales of large quantities of NGL, which can be absorbed into the market much more easily than LNG, must have improved. There have been reports of European petrochemical producers looking at NGL—and buying it—as a feedstock in preference to naphtha refined from crude oil, and it is no doubt significant that Kuwait, the first oil exporter to bring on stream one of the new generation

44

of NGL plants, has this year been raising its NGL prices. Similarly, at a time of crisis when the companies and consumer governments are anxious to secure crude oil supplies, there must be better prospects for sales of Middle Eastern refinery products and petrochemicals tied to crude oil allocations. This linkage is not something the Arabian governments like to talk about openly, but it is certainly an option available to them in their negotiations with individual purchasers and, in a more general sense, it will also affect the willingness of consumer governments to open their markets to Arabian industrial products in the face of inevitable opposition from unions and established producers at home.

Yet even with this general upturn in the prospects for Arabian heavy industry, it must be emphasized that heavy industrial revenues will never look very impressive financially as a supplement to oil incomes. At present oil and chemicals prices, the six Saudi petrochemical projects now at the advanced planning stage might not yield a revenue greater than that from 250,000 barrels a day of oil production—which is about 1/40th of current Saudi output.

Light industry

Most of the smaller manufacturing projects in the oil producing states in the last ten years have been set up by private investors, either through public companies or through private companies or partnerships. Although since 1976 there has been considerable government encouragement given through the cheap loans of the industrial development banks in Kuwait and Saudi Arabia, which account for almost all the region's light industry, the degree of private sector enthusiasm shown for industrial investment has been one of the surprises of Arabian development since the 1973—74 oil price explosion. By far the most popular type of project has been in building materials, although there have also been a number of investments in steel fabrication yards, simple food industries (notably flour milling) and industrial maintenance operations. In virtually every case the projects are designed to produce import substitutes rather than generate export revenues, although a few projects are now being built to cater for regional markets.

It seems likely that a fair number of the new industries, especially in Saudi Arabia, will go bankrupt. The Saudi policy has been to encourage the private sector to invest and not to be too strict about the economics of the projects to which it gives loans (at 2 per cent) through the Saudi Industrial Development Fund (SIDF). The idea is that even if quite a lot of projects do collapse a good number will succeed, and meanwhile the government does not have to worry too much about the money it may lose. As long as a project is regarded as being 'appropriate' for the kingdom—in other words not requiring too many imported labourers and standing at least a chance of being competitive with imports—it is more or less entitled to an SIDF loan as of right. (Occasionally SIDF loans have eventually been given to less competitive projects of which the government does not approve—a well known example being the Juffali-Daimler Benz plant for the assembly of Mercedes trucks.) Where the government is less prepared to offer support is with protection by tariffs which, if levied at all on industrial products coming into Saudi Arabia, are normally set at 20 per cent. Tariffs are unavoidably inflationary, and so protection will only be given if an otherwise desirable industry really needs it and is going to account for the greater proportion of the kingdom's demand for the product it manufactures.

The Arabian Peninsula is an unfavourable environment for light industry. There are all the extra capital and operating costs that afflict the heavy industries, including the need to house expatriate managers and technicians, pay them large salaries, fly them home once or twice a year and possibly pay for their children to be privately educated. Breakdowns occur more frequently, and take longer and cost more to repair, and there is always the possibility that the high rate of inflation in the oil states will make a project uncompetitive with imports between the time it is conceived and the time it is brought to fruition.

The problems are well illustrated by a notably successful company, Kirby Industries, originally a Houston firm which was bought outright by the Alghanim family in 1975 and which established its headquarters and a plant in Kuwait. The company had the built in advantage of manufacturing a product which could hardly help competing with imports: the steel frame building systems it makes, if imported from the USA, would have half of their cost accounted for by freight. From the first year the company made a profit, although since then its profits have grown more slowly than was hoped, and it has been particularly successful at penetrating export markets—it has even been considering exporting to China. And yet the profits earned in Kuwait have been substantially less than those from Kirby's continuing (and expanding) US operations, even though in America the company has to pay tax. Management has cost double what it costs in the USA, the inventory has to cover nine months compared to two weeks, the scrap factor is nine times as high because of a less able labour force, the Indian clerks at the middle and junior management levels have made expensive mistakes in every area of operations and, whereas in the USA the company could sell through hundreds of established outlets, in the Middle East it has had to develop a sales network of its own from scratch.

Kirby is saved by the huge freight cost of importing steel buildings and, as a general rule in the Middle East, it is the industries that save the customer paying freight to import by air that have been the most competitive. A good example of this has been SAPPCO, which manufactures plastic pipes in Riyadh and has been phenomenally profitable from the

46

start. It also helps if the industry is technically very simple, as are many building products industries. (Kirby's problems, of course, stem from its being a relatively complicated factory.) The relationship between freight advantage and complexity of manufacture is well illustrated by the experience of SAFAMI, a loss making fabricator of pipe systems for the oil and gas industries in Saudi Arabia. As a fairly rigid rule, SAFAMI has found that it has won contracts where the technical problems have been small and the freight costs high, but lost any contract where high quality work has been necessary. It is not that it cannot provide high quality, complicated work—it has imported welders from Texas—it just cannot do so competitively.

Although the experience of these companies presents a rather pessimistic picture overall, it does seem that conditions for light industry are gradually improving. Encouraged by industrial banks and the Gulf Organisation for Industrial Consulting, investors are now thinking of aiming their plants at the regional market rather than simply at their domestic markets. Now that the most obvious and most competitive industries, producing products for which there will be the biggest demand, have mostly been built, this regional orientation will be virtually a matter of necessity if new plants are to take advantage of economies of scale. It also seems likely that Arabian management and other Arab and Indian labour are gradually becoming more used to the demands of industry, and are therefore more efficient—particularly in their ability to avoid and repair breakdowns. And, as more and more industries and supporting service businesses are started up, there must be less need for each new plant to integrate vertically. Hitherto it has had to provide, at great expense to itself, its own service departments, its own repair tools, its own export sales outlets, etc., all of which have unavoidably spent much of their time lying idle. In future, in a more diverse economy, an industrial plant should be able to buy these services locally as and when it needs them.

Intermediate development stage

Neither light nor heavy industries in Arabia can be thought of as successes in the terms by which economic performance is normally judged. If the Arabian Peninsula were in imminent danger of running out of oil, or of finding its oil revenues inadequate for its spending, the poor performance of its industries would be a serious matter. As it is, the governments can afford to take a long term view: they believe that there is a clear logic in starting diversification early. There is the obvious pride in developing self-sufficiency and, meanwhile, what revenues are earned are not unwelcome. The present industries can be a training ground for the people who will launch the next phase of Arabian industrial development. As Dr Ghazi Algosaibi, the Saudi Industry Minister, has said, part of the purpose of the present generation of industries is to accustom some of the Saudi population to the routine of industrial life. Also the oil producers have to spend, and be seen to be spending, their money somehow—and although the pace of development may be considerably slowed following the social and religious troubles of the last year, this motive may still be as important as any other. Even if the projects are not perfect, what else can the producers do with their money except channel more and more into private hands, as discussed later?

Another aspect of the present diversification programmes is that there are just two cases where the new manufacturing and service industries are already playing, or soon might play, a genuinely important role in the national economy. The Bahrain government now draws some 40 per cent of its revenues from non-oil sources, while the net foreign income of ALBA and the offshore banking units alone are reckoned to contribute nearly a third as much foreign exchange as the state's oil revenues from all sources. (Bahrain not only has its own small field, it refines Saudi oil and receives half the revenues from a small offshore Saudi field.) If one includes invisible foreign exchange earnings from the dry dock, hotels and the whole leisure service centre business, it seems likely that over a third of Bahrain's total foreign exchange income is now being derived from sources other than oil.

The other country where diversification has an immediate relevance is Qatar. This state is at present perhaps more dependent on its oil income than any Arabian producer apart from Abu Dhabi, but clearly it is also going to be the next producer (after Bahrain) to find its oil income becoming inadequate for its spending. The day may be postponed by oil price rises, but meanwhile there is no doubt that the Qatar government is taking its heavy industry programme very seriously. The evidence shows in the state signing contracts, starting construction and bringing its post-1974 batch of industries to completion much more quickly than any other producer. As the Qataris see it, there is a risk that the alternative to their earning a significant industrial income ten years hence could be financial dependence on Saudi Arabia, which they would rather avoid.

But neither the Qatar nor the Bahrain cases alters the fact that for the Arabian oil producers as a whole revenue from diversification programmes is not going to be significant in volume or really essential for many years to come. (Bahrain and Qatar are also exceptional in being small states with relatively small needs for revenue, which means that income from diversification there has a better chance of making an impact than it does elsewhere.) The producers are realistic about their position. Although one often hears talk about building industries and developing the service side of the economy 'for the day when oil runs out', all of the present phase of diversification involves projects which run off oil or the disposal of oil income. The heavy industries use oil or associated natural gas as their feedstock and fuel; the light industries built so far are mostly intended to provide building materials for the oil financed development boom and depend on the cheap loans that oil revenues make possible; and the banking and foreign investment businesses that have grown up in Bahrain and Kuwait are geared either to financing imports and construction or disposing of private and government surpluses that stem from oil revenues. Apart from the badly mismanaged fishing business, and agricultural production in the major Saudi cases, there is very little economic activity in the Arabian Peninsula which would continue to make sense without oil. One must see the diversification schemes so far as being an intermediate stage, on the foundations of which governments hope there will eventually grow a new economy, of a shape as yet undefined, which will sustain Arabia in the post-oil era.

Unassociated gas

The only important exception to these comments may be natural gas. All of the gas being exploited in Arabia at present is associated gas, dissolved in oil or found as a cap on top of oil reservoirs, and this obviously has a life as long as the life of the oilfields; but recently there have been discoveries of unassociated gas. This gas, found on its own at depths much greater than oil in the Middle East, is still something of an unknown quantity, although the drilling done so far gives grounds for optimism. Major fields have been discovered, although not yet fully appraised, in Iran, Abu Dhabi and Qatar, while Aramco says that wherever it has done deep drilling it has struck gas. The company's employees are prepared to suggest unofficially that wherever there is a suitable reservoir formation at the deep Khuff levels where gas has been found so far, there will indeed turn out to be a gasfield. This applies in the major Saudi oil producing area from south Ghawar to Qatif. Nowhere is the development of these gasfields being pushed ahead as yet, mainly because there is no financial urgency to do so and no very big established trade in LNG into which the new fields could be fitted without difficulty. When the unassociated gas is developed it will not necessarily be possible to substitute it for associated gas in the present gas based heavy industries such as petrochemicals and fertilizers; both the calorific value and the content of unassociated gas (in terms of proportions of methane, ethane and NGL) is generally different from that of associated gases. Nor may it be that unassociated gas reserves will last very much longer than oil. However, the development of these reserves would count as an industrial diversification (of a sort) which right from the start would yield a revenue entirely independent from that of oil production.

The super-rich society

Ironically, at the same time as the Arabian oil producers have been trying to diversify their sources of income over the last ten or twenty years, they have been pursuing another policy which can only make diversifications more difficult and put off the day when their economies might be self-sufficient without oil revenues. This has been the wholesale enrichment of their own citizens. The richer the population become the more dependent they must be on a high oil income to maintain the standard of living to which they have made themselves accustomed, and the less prepared they are to forsake the easy lives of landlord or driver for the more demanding routine of manager or industrial shift worker. One might say that the oil producers have set themselves the almost impossible task of not only diversifying, but diversifying while maintaining their people as some of the richest in the world.

The people of the Arabian oil states, or at least some of the Arabian oil states, are rich not only in the technical statistical sense of appearing to have the highest per capita incomes when their states' oil revenues are divided by numbers of population. They are rich in the real personal sense of having the world's highest disposable incomes and living in the world's most generous welfare states.

Per capita income as normally calculated is a rather meaningless figure because it gives all residents of the state the same average income, whereas in practice there is no averagely wealthy person in Arabia: in Kuwait, Qatar and Abu Dhabi especially there are rich nationals and mostly poor immigrants. In Bahrain, Saudi Arabia and Oman the picture is slightly different in so far as these states have some relatively poor nationals as well as poor foreigners. Bahrain and Oman both have had oil revenues too small to enable them to embark on the wholesale enrichment of their people, and Saudi Arabia was in much the same position up to 1973. In its first twenty-five years of oil production, Saudi Arabia's cumulative revenues came to no more than Kuwait's, although they had to be spread over a vastly greater country and much bigger population. In Saudi Arabia there has also been an ideological objection to making the enrichment of citizens an end in itself. This was certainly the view held in King Faisal's day and embodied in the Second Five Year Plan, which states that its principle social objective would be to assure all Saudis '. . . an adequate dignified minimum standard of living. Levels above this minimum will continue to be the reward of individual effort and achievement.' Under the pressure of raised popular expectations, however, the present Saudi rulers seem to have allowed themselves to slide towards the enrichment philosophy, probably without making a formal decision for or against it.

Although the philosophy may not be pursued with equal thoroughness in all countries, there are a number of spending policies and pieces of business and social legislation which one comes to recognize as being peculiarly 'Arabian oil state' in character. They are ingeniously designed to pump real personal wealth into the hands of citizens while giving non-citizens enough to induce them to stay and perform their useful work but no more.

In Kuwait, which has the most comprehensive enrichment policies and is therefore the most commonly quoted example, the major means of distributing wealth has been through the purchase of land at inflated prices. The exact mechanics of land buying have varied from area to area according to time and circumstances. Typically, the state buys land at the market price or slightly over, zones it, installs services and infrastructure and then leases it or sells it off for further development or private houses for only slightly more than it paid in the first place. From the point of view of the relatively 'poor' Kuwaiti, this may involve his selling land in one area at a high price and then being sold land with services provided in a lower price area elsewhere—at the same time as being given a cheap loan with which to build a house. (His capital profit on the land transaction he can invest.) In fact, government sales of land are relatively uncommon. Normally the government leases back the land, which means that the state now owns about 90 per cent of the land in Kuwait City and ensures that the flow of capital is mostly one way. In other countries, and particularly in Saudi Arabia where the modern state has grown out of a less settled community, most of the land has been vested from the start in the hands of the ruling family, and has been used for gifts to subjects whom the family has wanted to reward. In all countries urban land prices and rents are extremely high because the expansion of the economy and the growth of population seems to have outstripped the rate at which services have been provided for new land. In all countries, too, only nationals may own land or buildings, which gives them a monopoly of rent income from expatriates, and in most countries there are housing banks which provide house-holders and developers with very cheap building loans. Occasionally there have been cases of all outstanding loans being written off by governments that are anxious for political or economic reasons to make a gesture of goodwill towards their people. There are free housing schemes almost everywhere for the 'poorest' citizens.

To complement these policies, Arabian governments pay extremely generous salaries for jobs that often require nominal effort or perfunctory attendance, although traditionally the Saudis have been less generous than the Kuwaitis. There are virtually no taxes or social security contributions to be paid. Among the few exceptions applied to non-foreigners are the religious tax, *zakat*, which is a semi-optional levy of 2½ per cent on the increase in a man's assets over a year, a few indirect taxes levied on imports to protect local manufacturers, and a small Kuwaiti corporation tax which companies have to pay to a fund for scientific advancement. Income tax and purchase taxes of any sort so far have been unthinkable.

Education is free everywhere, with governments paying the tuition fees and (extremely generous) pocket money of students who qualify to go to university abroad. Health services likewise are mostly free—although the much publicised King Faisal Hospital in Riyadh is a private establishment. Once again, governments pay for patients who need specialist treatment to be sent to hospital abroad, and they also pay the expenses of the relations who accompany the patient. In most states internal telephone calls are free, although water can be quite expensive. Most of this particular category of welfare policies benefits the whole community, although foreigners do not get paid for when they go abroad to university or to hospital.

In commerce, the oil states help their citizens by confining to them alone the ownership of shares in public companies, and in most cases insisting that nationals have at least 51 per cent of any private business. As with housing, cheap loans are provided for industrialists and contractors, although in Saudi Arabia foreign partners are also eligible for loans as long as their share in a business is below a certain level. In the emirates, Saudi Arabia and Qatar the state also seems reasonably happy to tolerate huge commissions being paid by foreign companies to agents who help them win government contracts—even though commissions on occasions have put up contract prices by over 20 per cent. Kuwait seems to suffer less from this sort of practice, although it has often been prepared to bale out private sector businessmen who have run into trouble—giving them loans or buying the shares of the companies they have launched. The most recent example of this policy in operation came at the end of 1977 when the Kuwait government launched a buying operation to support prices on the Kuwaiti stock exchange.

Taken as a whole the enriching policies have made the Arabians addicted to a type of life which only oil revenues on a vast scale (which fortunately is likely to continue) can make possible. They have also made them much more dependent on immigrants than they would have been in societies with less generous spending policies; it was calculated recently in Kuwait that every Kuwaiti national born is going to need two and a half immigrants to run the economy off which he lives. It is often said that immigrants are necessary for their technical and managerial skills and because the indigenous populations of the oil states have been simply too small in numbers to operate a modern economy. In reality, this is only half of the story. The fact that the enriching policies have been easiest to focus on two areas of activity—trade and land—has meant that those eligible for enrichment, i.e. citizens, have gravitated to these two activities. Many Arabians are perfectly capable and well enough educated to pursue careers in the professions, government service, state corporations or industrial management. Others—the

52

driver, doorman, tea boy class—are quite capable of working as labourers or learning a skill. The fact that only a very few of either class chooses to take up these options is partly a matter of cultural tradition, but also a matter of the rewards being greater, or the life being easier for the same reward elsewhere.

Two questions have emerged from the enrichment policies over the last five years. The first, broadly speaking, has been how effective are they? And the second has been, should they be continued?

In Kuwait the enrichment policies have been so thorough, and have been in operation for so long, that the first question does not arise. But elsewhere, governments have been worried by the feeling that high rates of inflation, caused by overspending producing bottlenecks, may have made their established policies inadequate. There has been no doubt at all that the gap between the richest and the 'poorest' has widened and there are fears that the high expectations created among all citizens by the oil price explosion may not have been fulfilled. In Saudi Arabia there has been a drift from the villages into the big towns, and those who have not made a success of their new lives as drivers, lorry owners or minor contractors must be disillusioned. Their jealousies must have been sharpened by the nature of the Arabian market place, where the 'buyer beware' philosophy is unchallenged and where merchants will exploit any temporary monopoly or tightness in the market to the greatest possible degree. In Arabia there is not the constraint that there is on Western corporations of exposure of excessive profits or racketeering damaging a company's image.

In all the Arabian oil producers these strains have been added to the normal social strains of fast growth in the region. The governments' spending programmes have led to an influx of Arab and non-Arab immigrants and visitors, who may or may not represent a security risk but who certainly do introduce alien cultural influences. Governments' spending also changes the jobs, lives and routines of their citizens, it enables them to go abroad, and the cash it puts in their pockets gives them Western material aspirations. Originally it was feared that these changes would lead to demands for greater political participation and the erosion of the family, now the fear is of parts of the population rejecting the Western influence to which they have been exposed and becoming involved in the 'Muslim revival' which produced the occupation of the Mecca mosque and the riots in the Saudi Eastern Province and in Bahrain.

Even before the economies settled down to more modest rates of growth in the last year or so, the economic malaise in Arabian society never reached anything like the intensity that it did in Iran. The economic mismanagement had been less serious, the rural—urban drift had taken place on a smaller scale, slower down spending did not not seem to cause unemployment (and certainly not unemployment among the

53

people who mattered—the citizens) and, most important, the governments had the money directly to alleviate their peoples' problems on a scale that the Iranians could not match. It was in their response to inflation and their fears of a disillusioned citizenry that the Saudis moved towards the 'absolute welfare' enrichment policies of the richer Gulf states. All Arabian oil state governments began subsidizing staple foods, either by setting price controls and paying subsidies to the traditional importers, or by setting up their own loss making 'supply companies' and issuing all residents (not just citizens) with ration books. They also raised salaries in government service and the armed forces, set profit controls on non-food consumer imports (although these were widely ignored), passed legislation on permissable commissions for agents negotiating any sort of contract (also ineffective) and fixed prices for the output of local industries and utilities. In Saudi Arabia at one point the government decreed a 60 per cent cut in the electricity tariff and subsidized the producers' losses. In Bahrain, where such lavish subsidies have been beyond the government's means, the state has introduced compulsory employers' social security contributions.

In future it seems likely that Arabian governments will spend more slowly so as to control inflation and restrain the growth of excessive expectations. In Saudi Arabia there will probably be more emphasis put on rural spending, including the development of agriculture, in order to half the drift to the towns and keep people more insulated from modern cultural influences. (There are also directly social, as opposed to economic, considerations dictating slower spending, but these fall slightly outside the scope of this chapter.)

The other question sometimes heard in Arabia recently—concerning whether the enrichment policies should be continued—may seem at first to be a direct contradiction of the governments' concern with preventing the economic disillusionment of their subjects. (In fact, the question applies mainly to policies which actively enrich citizens, rather than to the alleviation of the effects of inflation.) Furthermore, it is being asked mainly in Kuwait, whose citizens are in a different league of wealth from most of the other Arabians, and it must be admitted that even in Kuwait the question is only raised occasionally and in a fairly tentative form.

The main questioner so far as been Abdel-Rahman Atiqi, the Finance Minister, who has spoken against the government's tendency to always bale out public and private sector 'lame ducks', and has even mentioned once or twice that eventually citizens will themselves have to play a role in supporting their government by paying taxes, as people do elsewhere in the world. (Most of Atiqi's motives in making his occasional remarks have been to prepare Kuwaitis psychologically for the day when they will have to pay tax.) In practical terms, all that has happened in Kuwait has been a tightening up on the payment of tax by foreign companies in joint ventures and the introduction of a 5 per cent corporate profits tax, paid to the Fund for Scientific Advancement. This tax is not part of the law but in practice it seems to be compulsory. In Bahrain there has been the social security contributions law, which is gradually being extended to embrace smaller companies.

Arabian businessmen would be quite right in seeing these new rules as the thin end of a wedge. It will be done very gradually but governments will want to establish the principle of tax well in advance of their actually needing internal finance to supplement their oil revenues. For social reasons they will also want increasingly to regulate profits and the brutal code of Arabian business practice. Commercial life will become more and more subject to the type of regulation that is taken for granted in the West. The business community may resist the changes, as the Bahrain merchants resisted the introduction of a commercial registration fee early in 1977 and got the amount halved from $10,000 annually to $5,000, but slowly the Arabians will be asked to undertake a big adjustment of their view of the state. Instead of thinking of it as a provider of all things, they will have to see it as an institution that they themselves have a duty partially to support.

Basic data on oil producers

Saudi Arabia: *Oil revenues 1978:* $37 billion
Oil reserves: 166 billion barrels
Production 1978: 8.3 million barrels a day
Reserves/production ratio: 55 years
Start of production: 1939, restarted 1946
Population: 6.5 million (2 million immigrants)

Kuwait: *Oil revenues 1978:* $9.5 billion
Oil reserves: 66 billion barrels
Production 1978: 1.9 million barrels a day
Reserves/production ratio: 97 years
Start of oil production: 1946
Population: 1.5 million (0.8 million immigrants)

Bahrain: *Oil revenues 1978:* $0.4 billion
Oil reserves: 0.25 billion barrels
Production 1978: 0.06 million barrels a day
Reserves/production ratio: 12 years
Start of oil production: mid 1930s
Population: 300,000 (100,000 immigrants)

NOTE: Bahrain already draws some 40 per cent of its state revenues from sources other than oil. Unlike the highly affluent people of the other Arabian oil states, its relatively well educated citizens are prepared to take industrial and junior management jobs: at times the government has had to pursue formal job creating policies because it has been unable to adopt the enrichment policies of other Arabian countries. Many Bahrainis wear Western dress rather than the *thobe*, which has become tne self-conscious distinguishing uniform of the other Arabians.

To help Bahrain's sources of income other Arabian countries, notably Saudi Arabia, appear to have avoided competing with some of Bahrain's development schemes. The Saudis share the revenues of an offshore oilfield with Bahrain and have held back on their own aluminium project, while the Kuwaitis have avoided competing with Bahrain's offshore banking units. OAPEC has located its dry dock in Bahrain, and the island has long been the headquarters of Gulf Air (owned by all the lower Gulf states and Oman)—not that there would have been any competitors for the base when the airline was set up. However, there have been some exceptions to this pattern of good neighbourliness. Dubai has its own dry dock and aluminium smelter, and the UAE's equivalent of offshore banking units have had their development held back not by government policy but by the lack of international confidence in the UAE banking system.

Qatar: *Oil revenues 1978:* $2.2 billion
                  Oil reserves: 4 billion barrels
                  Production 1978: 0.48 million barrels a day
                  Reserves/production ratio: 23 years
                  Start of oil production: 1949
                  Population: 170,000 (120,000 immigrants)

Abu Dhabi: *Oil revenues 1978:* $7 billion
                  Oil reserves: 30 billion barrels
                  Production 1978: 1.45 million barrels a day
                  Reserves/production ratio: 57 years
                  Start of oil production: 1962 (development began 1966)
                  Population: 280,000 (230,000 immigrants)

Dubai: *Oil revenues 1978:* $1.7 billion
                  Oil reserves: 1.3 billion barrels
                  Production 1978: 0.36 million barrels a day
                  Reserves/production ratio: 10 years
                  Start of oil production: 1969
                  Population: 280,000 (220,000 immigrants)

Oman: *Oil revenues 1978:* $1.7 billion
                  Oil reserves: 2.5 billion barrels
                  Production 1978: 0.32 million barrels a day
                  Reserves/production ratio: 22 years
                  Start of oil production: 1958
                  Population: 1 million (200,000 immigrants)

4 Population, migration and development in the Gulf states
Allan G. Hill

Introduction

Between the five 'city states' of the Gulf (Kuwait, Qatar, the United Arab Emirates, Bahrain and Oman) and the three larger units (Iran, Iraq and Saudi Arabia) there are obviously significant differences in size, in wealth, in type of economic development and hence in population characteristics.[1] The oil dominated economies of the smaller states have expanded rapidly in the post-1945 period using imported labour principally from the other Arab countries but also from Asia (the Indian sub-continent), Europe and North America. At present, the main period of immigration, at least of the 'semi-permanent' kind where dependants accompany the workers and remain there for many years, appears to be over and more of the growth of the immigrant populations in the city states is now due to natural increase rather than to immigration. These natural increase rates for citizens and aliens alike have now reached very high levels due to a combination of rapidly reduced mortality and almost unaltered levels of fertility. In the larger oil states, immigration has never been as important politically or socially as elsewhere in the Gulf simply because the immigrants, although numerous, amount to only a smaller fraction of the total population. Natural increase rates in Iran, Iraq and Saudi Arabia are a little lower than in the smaller oil states due to a slower decline in mortality but the growth rates of these larger populations are still high, producing a substantial numerical increase in the total population each year.

---

1 All eight countries are subsequently referred to as 'Gulf countries'; the five smaller units including Saudi Arabia are referred to as 'Gulf states'.

There are thus two different sets of population based problems faced by the two groups of Gulf countries. The five smaller countries and Saudi Arabia have to find ways of continuing their past economic expansion, based as it is on the use of substantial amounts of expatriate labour. In addition to arranging the continuous supply of new foreign labour, they have to supervise the composition and growth of the existing immigrant communities which, because of their now quite long established position in the Gulf states, are growing at high rates of natural increase. Their own national populations are also expanding very rapidly and creating an annual addition of youngsters which even rich oil states are finding difficulty in absorbing, especially when compounded by the growing numbers of children of immigrants with similar needs for schooling, health care and the like. The larger oil states, by comparison, have a much smaller problem of immigration although Saudi Arabia, despite its larger population and area, still experiences many of the immigration problems faced by the smaller states. Even Iraq and Iran are dependent on skilled foreign workers in certain key sectors of the economy, notably oil. The problems in these larger countries are basically the conventional ones faced by most developing countries—rapid population growth running ahead of balanced economic growth and of service provision for the expanding populations. In the oil states, of course, the level of service provision desired or considered acceptable is very much higher than in most non-oil developing countries and this sector is an extensive user of labour. An additional problem in the larger states is that the indigenous populations are not homogeneous in religion, language and ethnic background. Hence, problems related to the geographic distribution and national aspirations of the minorities are as important as the balance between the citizens and the immigrants which is of major concern to the smaller countries of the Gulf.

This paper concentrates principally on the demographic and related economic and political problems faced by the oil states of Arabia, but some specific population problems facing Iraq and Iran are also considered.

The demographic situation in the late 1970s

Whilst there is considerable variation in the size of the populations of the Gulf countries (Table 4.1), all are part of the high fertility region of south-west Asia. With the exception of Iran, there appears to be no well established downward trend in fertility in any of the other seven countries either amongst the nationals or among the resident alien populations. The combination of falling mortality and almost unchanged fertility results in very high rates of natural increase.

Table 4.1

Population size and growth rates in the states surrounding the Gulf

	Area ('000 KM²)	Estimated mid 1979 population ('000)	Proportion of total population foreigners (%)	Estimated annual population growth rate (%)	Proportion of total population urban (%)
Bahrain	.6	285	13.9	3.4	80
Iran	1,648.0	46,462	0.5	3.0	44
Iraq	434.9	12,812	4.0	3.1	62
Kuwait	17.8	1,262	52.5	5.9	89
Oman	212.4	867	25.0	3.2	5
Qatar	11.0	239	61.8	8.5	88
Saudi Arabia	2,149.7	8,396	21.0	3.6	21
United Arab Emirates	83.6	883	70.0	11.4	84

Note: The population totals have been estimated by projecting forwards from the last census year using known rates of growth. These growth rates are not well established in Qatar, the UAE and Oman; in Oman, with no complete census, the figures are very approximate.

60

There appears to be a well established pattern of demographic evolution to which all the Gulf states tend to conform. It begins during the time that oil is first discovered with high mortality conditions and quite high levels of fertility associated with early and almost universal marriage. Following the beginning of work on the first major development plan, heavy investments are usually made in the health sector with the result that adult mortality begins to decline. Next the problem of infant and childhood mortality is tackled and special efforts are made to improve the conditions of childbearing and then to ensure that more of the newborn survive by improving feeding practices and by dealing with the most common causes of childhood death. This point has been reached by all the Gulf countries but at different times. Kuwait and Bahrain are probably the most advanced because of a combination of their small size and the early discovery and development of oil. Iran and Saudi Arabia are taking longer to pass through the same stages simply because of their larger size.

At a later stage a few elite families start to reduce their high fertility levels by a combination of later marriage and the deliberate control of marital fertility. This lower level of fertility prevails amongst women with a secondary level of education or above and so the onset of a more general fertility decline is related to the productivity of the educational system. An important question is therefore whether the education system can do more than keep pace with larger cohorts so that the educational levels of the female population as a whole rise steadily in the future.

It is possible to plot the progress of the Gulf states through these stages. It is interesting to note that there is a kind of 'wave' effect sweeping down the Gulf roughly in step with the first export of significant amounts of oil.

The rates of natural increase for the immigrant communities of the Gulf are more difficult to fit into this overall pattern simply because the immigrants themselves come from a very diverse set of origins. Certainly, many young male migrants from surrounding Middle Eastern countries migrate to save money with marriage in mind but it is much harder to see a simple connection between income and fertility for those already married who live and work in the Gulf. An obvious key factor affecting the fertility of the immigrants is whether they are unaccompanied males or not. The well established immigrant groups have fertility and mortality levels which match the levels of the nationals although, in some cases, fertility amongst the immigrants appears to be even higher than that of the nationals (e.g. the Palestinians in Kuwait). With much reduced levels of net immigration in recent years in most Gulf states, the growth of the immigrant populations due to natural increase assumes a much greater numerical significance.

Immigration itself has also passed through a number of states in the

Gulf countries as the economies of each have grown and matured. At the outset, soon after the discovery of oil, the kind of labour needed was a small number of highly skilled engineers and technicians and a larger number of semi-skilled workers primarily in the oil sector. To meet these needs, expatriates from the West were imported to fill the first category and, for the second, workers were brought from India and Pakistan. At least one oil company had a recruiting station in Bombay to provide a supply of foremen and clerks.

Unskilled labour came from the local population or from the Arab countries nearby. Persian workers crossed the Gulf in large numbers at an early stage to work in Arabia. As the development of the country got under way, the demands for unskilled labour increased dramatically since the expansion of each country's economy invariably began with a dramatic growth in construction activity. At about this time (the early 1950s in Kuwait, later in the lower Gulf) the refugees from Palestine provided a ready source of unskilled and semi-skilled labour. Some Arabs from the northern Arab countries quickly established strong business footholds and others became influential in government or in the professions. Both the refugees and others in the professions had good reasons for bringing their dependants with them—the first group had no choice apart from leaving them in refugee camps and the second group had the resources and the established position which made them feel comfortable with their new life in the Gulf. Thus, the migrant flow from the Arab countries quickly changed from being a purely male flow to one in which children and women were present in significant proportions. On the other hand, the immigrants from the Yemens, Iran, Oman, Sudan and other poor countries to the south has remained a largely male influx. The turnover of this last group of migrants is very high since they return home at not more than annual intervals and they are replaced by migrants from the same origins with approximately the same characteristics.

The most recent development has been for the oil states to move away from the traditional sources of labour and turn to Asians in increasing numbers. The advantages of Asian labour is first that it is cheaper; the introduction of Asians into Saudi Arabia (Pakistanis and workers from south east Asia including the Philippines) has driven down wage rates and led to the return migration of some North Yemeni workers as a result. An additional attraction of the labour from Asia is that workers generally leave their dependants at home so that there is less pressure to provide social and other services for immigrants. The males can therefore be accommodated in rather frugal 'work camps'. Finally, it seems that Asian contractors are offering contracts which include the import, use and then the export of labour at the end of the contract. The South Koreans encourage this way of working since it helps to recapture a larger fraction of the workers's remittances in the domestic economy as the workers are paid in Korea in local currency. Several major projects in the Gulf, including the OAPEC dry dock in Bahrain have been built in this way, usually ahead of schedule.

Urbanization and its consequences

The cities of the Middle East have always been dominant in the economic, political and religious life of the region. Recently, they have also come to dominate numerically because of rapid rates of natural increase of the urban populations combined with substantial migration into the cities from rural areas. In general, about half of the recent population growth of Middle Eastern cities is due to migration and half to the excess of births over deaths. Between 1970 and 1975, the urban population of the region grew at an average of 5.2 per cent per annum and many individual cities grew much more rapidly. Between 1963 and 1974, for example, Riyadh's population jumped from 159,000 to 667,000, Jeddah grew from 147,000 to 561,000 and smaller towns like Taif, Medina and Hofuf at least doubled in size. As a result, well over half of all Middle Easterners now live in towns and cities and this fraction is increasing steadily, leading to a clear reduction in the numbers working in the agricultural sector. The already heavy reliance of the Gulf countries on imported meat, grains and even dairy produce is increasing further as a result; even tastes have changed, moving away from domestically produced foodstuffs in favour of the imported substitutes.

The bulk of urban employment in the Gulf countries is in the service sector, especially in professional and personal services. High wages have attracted labour from other sectors and driven up the price of labour in agriculture and industry. Finding skilled and semi-skilled production workers from within the domestic labour markets in the Gulf is very difficult which means that long term plans for industrial development and diversification even in the larger countries (Iraq, Iran and Saudi Arabia) look rather bleak.

The cities themselves now consist of a heterogeneous mix of peoples frequently living in separate quarters from one another. The restrictions on foreigners owning land and property in most Gulf countries have produced a fairly strict system of residential segregation between citizens and immigrants. This may be one factor responsible for the almost negligible amount of intercommunal violence in the Gulf states. But in Iraq and Iran especially, the flood of rural—urban migrants has produced large areas of squatter housing which form a marked contrast to the smart villas and apartments of the established urban middle class. The juxtaposition of rich and poor in the city appears to have brought about comparatively little class resentment on the part of the 'have nots', possibly because large inequalities in income distribution have always been a feature of the region or because the inequalities are not expressed in class terms. Nevertheless, the immigrant from Khuzistan in Tehran or from Amara in Baghdad does feel some antipathy to a system which apparently looks after him so badly. The half-finished land reform process in Iraq and Iran forced many peasants into cities and any suggestion that those in power support these erstwhile landlords and shaikhs inevitably produces feelings of bitterness. The neglect of the rural areas where daily wages for a labourer can still be less than one-tenth of those in Baghdad or Tehran contributes to the continuing rural exodus and to the growing potential problem of large numbers of disaffected people in the major cities.

It is remarkable that despite the concentration of people in urban areas social change and modernization have not proceeded more rapidly. (Even today, very few urban women work outside the house and attitudes to women and children appear to have changed very little.) High fertility seems as important a goal as any even amongst the lower classes, a group one would expect to be most constrained by resources in an urban setting. It is especially hard to explain this effect in the Gulf states where the higher status immigrants (Europeans and northern area Arabs) have displayed 'modern' attitudes and behaviour. Perhaps it is because the modern mercantile type of economy does not require a drastic break from the past, being essentially based on family and kinship as before, or perhaps the Gulf nationals are retreating behind their traditional values to avoid total absorption by the imported variety. Whatever the explanation, the economic and political consequences of retaining the older values include an increased dependence on foreign labour (if women are not in the labour force) and a lack of capacity in certain areas (the less pleasant maintenance jobs in engineering, for example). A possibly offsetting political consideration is that by adopting a traditional posture on social and religious matters, the ruling elites are less likely to be identified with the West if there is a backlash from the disgruntled masses in the shantytowns of the major cities.

Immigration

During the search for oil and thereafter when oil exporting began, important differences emerged between the Gulf states which considerably affected the character and volume of the immigrant flows. First, the timing of the oil discoveries had a bearing on subsequent developments; for example, the decision by the allies to focus production, export and refining efforts on Bahrain during the Second World War meant that Bahrain got an early start at the expense of countries like Kuwait—despite the former's meagre total reserves. The pattern of discovery also affected the timing of oil developments for it took some time to appreciate that the whole Gulf region was a massive oil reservoir after the early discoveries had been made in the Zagros mountains in Iran around 1908. Thus, we find that in the 1970s the lower Gulf states shared many of the attributes of Kuwait in the 1950s. Whereas the Kuwaitis were looking for skilled immigrants in the 1970s, since one of their several construction booms had been completed, the lower Gulf states were still demanding large numbers of construction workers and unskilled labour.

Secondly, the magnitude of the oil reserves discovered has had a profound affect on the character of subsequent developments. Compare the neighbouring countries of Bahrain and Qatar; the Bahrainis, because of their small oil reserves, quickly turned to oil and gas processing industries which gave them an introduction to the engineering industry in general. This led to Bahrain becoming a service and repair centre for the whole of the Gulf region, especially for companies operating in the offshore zone. Qatar, on the other hand, after oil exporting began in 1949, discovered and produced more and more oil as time went by and concern about seeking alternative sources of revenue evaporated when the ageing Dukhan field was supplemented by new discoveries offshore.

Thirdly, some countries in the Gulf had developed longstanding ties with countries outside the Gulf prior to the discovery of oil. Political responsibility for the Gulf states was passed from the government of India to the British Foreign Office as recently as 1949 and the connections with the Indian sub-continent have been preserved by the lower Gulf states through trade and exchange of people. Each of these factors helps to explain the different nationality 'mix' found in each of the labour importing countries.

Another factor of considerable importance affecting the character and direction of the migrant stream was the establishment of the state of Israel. This coincided with the beginning of a period of very rapid economic growth in the Gulf (especially Kuwait) so that the obvious place where the displaced Palestinians could find work was the Gulf. Many migrated on a temporary basis but soon found that return to Palestine was impossible. In 1970, for example, 33 per cent of the Jordanians and Palestinians in Kuwait had been there for ten years or more. Other states in the Gulf were slower to develop and were in any case wary of the political implications of admitting Palestinians. The lower Gulf states had access to the pool of cheap labour from India and Pakistan and so admitted very few Palestinians. It seems that Saudi Arabia also preferred Asians to Palestinians although the reasons for this preference are not clear.

Considering the length of the unpatrolled boundaries and the attractiveness of the wage rates in the Gulf countries, the surprising thing is that the influx of migrants, both workers and dependants, has not been larger. The principal reason whey the flow has not swamped the smaller countries is the emergence of a strong system of regional co-operation between the labour exporters and the labour importers. As part of a system of control, most of the oil states introduced nationality and labour laws which first defined the native national population in terms which excluded the post-oil immigrants and then gave preference to nationals in employment and in a host of other fields. Only nationals can own property and businesses in the oil states, for example, and immigrants are excluded from certain grades in the civil service and are discriminated against in the provision of social welfare benefits and the supply of other services.

Nonetheless, the post-1973 oil price rises started another boom in the economies of the oil states which meant increased demands for imported labour and it was the result of this boom which has led many labour exporting countries to become seriously worried about skilled manpower shortages in their own economies. The oil states themselves have begun to turn to Asian sources of labour due to a combination of high prices and shortage of supply from the usual Arab labour sending countries. Use of Asian labour may introduce a new set of problems for the control of immigration in the oil states but, in the short term, the use of indentured labour brought in by contractors from east Asia relieves the labour importers from some of the worries they have over the control of, for example, Yemeni and Pakistani workers and their dependants.

Every labour importing country in the Gulf requires migrants to obtain a visa and a work permit prior to immigration. This entails production of a document from an employer offering a migrant a job and assuming legal responsibility for that person. The migrants' immediate dependants are usually granted visitor or residence permits on application once the migrant is established in his or her new place of work. There are some parts of the economy where these rules cannot be so strictly applied, e.g. domestic servants and day labourers in the ports or in the construction industry. From time to time, illegal migrants are deported in considerable numbers but, in most cases, the illegal immigration of male unskilled labourers does not pose any threat to the security of the national economy since these workers are highly mobile and are unlikely to become a major charge on the public services because they are unaccompanied men and also because they do not use these services as they are nervous about being detected as illegal entrants.

In general, then, a system for the control of regional movements of people has grown up which is quite efficient at curtailing the enormous numbers of migrants who would undoubtedly otherwise enter the oil producing states. The system is based on the self-interest of labour exporters and of labour importers which appear to broadly coincide at present although there are signs of friction both in the labour exporting and in the labour importing countries. The importers are concerned about the size of their immigrant communities and at the way some national groups have a hold on certain sectors of the economy (see p.   ). The labour exporters feel that their own development plans are suffering from the loss of skilled workers abroad and they are also aware of some of the problems their workers are facing in the oil exporting states. Recent moves by the Egyptians to restrict the movement of single women to Arabia and growing complaints about the systems of discrimination between citizens and immigrants are signs of growing disenchantment with the existing arrangements. At the core of the difficulties is the issue of the very restrictive nationality laws enacted by all the Gulf states.

Nationality quotas

None of the labour importing countries have explicit nationality quotas except that in most countries, Iran excluded, Arab workers and migrants are given preference over non-Arabs by the labour and nationality laws. In practice, every country watches very closely the total numbers and composition of its foreign population and from time to time takes steps to control further immigration from one or more sources, or even to allow the numbers from one country to decline by repatriation or by reducing the number of new entry permits. External political events (e.g. the threatened takeover of Kuwait by Iraq in 1961 and the 1967 Arab-Israeli war) affect both the flow and return of migrants and official attitudes to migrants from a single source. Palestinians have suffered from systematic discrimination in almost every Arab country except Kuwait. The Palestinian communities in Abu Dhabi and Saudi Arabia are newly established and have yet to acquire the same dominant status as they have in Kuwait.

A problem faced by all Gulf countries is that some immigrants from the northern Arab countries, once established, introduce their dependants and start behaving like a settled population by having children, demanding housing, education and other services. Other nationalities have a much higher turnover rate since they may specialize in the supply of certain grades of labour. Thus, it is relatively easy to predict the future composition of the immigrant community given a certain amount of information about future development projects. For a large construction programme, for example, Kuwait knows that it will need labour normally supplied by Oman, Yemen and Egypt for the heavy manual tasks. To staff a new hospital, some Arab doctors and nurses may be found but it will probably be necessary to turn to India or Pakistan or even to recruit from the Philippines. To expand the education system, on the other hand, teachers will probably be recruited from Jordan, Palestine, Egypt, Syria and Lebanon.

The result of this policy of controlling immigration and the immigrants very closely is that 'enclaves' build up. Suburbs in Kuwait have become almost independent units in which the residents are supported by work carried out for Kuwaitis, but in their offices and in their homes live separate lives from the national population. The same can be said of some of the major new industrial cities developing elsewhere in Saudi Arabia. Yenbo and Jubail, for example, will be industrial enclaves built and operated by expatriates but with presumably Saudi managers in key positions.

Naturalization

A key part of the legislation developed in the Gulf states to control migration is the law on naturalization. At an early stage in each country's development, a decision was taken not to offer nationality to new immigrants. In Kuwait, for example, legislation was introduced in 1948, just two years after the start of oil exporting. In part, the rulers of the Gulf states made this decision out of a genuine fear that they would be overwhelmed by a flood of immigrants from the more populous Arab countries and from India and Pakistan. However, there were other components in the decision. One of them was the Arab League decision that the Palestinian refugees would not be naturalized and absorbed by other Arab countries. Another seems to have been an early acceptance that they would rather employ foreigners to do the manual, technical and non-administrative jobs in the economy despite the dependence on outsiders which this would produce. Only if the new arrivals could be effectively identified and dominated would the system be acceptable and reasonably secure. Thus the policy which has emerged of discrimination against the immigrants in every walk of life has to be seen as an essential part of the development of every Gulf state. Without the security brought about by 'separate development' of the native and immigrant communities in the Gulf, the political independence and stability of each of the small Gulf states would be seriously threatened. However, there are vested interests on both sides in maintaining stability and prosperity in the Gulf so that the injustices inherent in the system are rarely fully aired or translated into sustained demands for improvement or serious political activity.

Most Arab countries will allow foreigners, especially Arabs, to apply for nationality after four to five years of residence but in the Gulf the conditions attached to naturalization are much more severe. Kuwait, for example, requires fifteen years of continuous residence and, even on naturalization, excludes the newly naturalized from having certain political rights. The Kuwaiti law only permits a maximum of fifty naturalizations in any one year although, in practice, Badu (Bedouin) and others from the bordering countries are given passports following a period of service in the army or the police force. The new nationals carry distinct identity cards.

In the UAE, Arabs from Qatar, Oman and Bahrain are granted citizenship after only three years of residence (ten years for Arabs from other countries). Again, the newly naturalized are excluded from full rights of citizenship for the first seven years after naturalization. Of all the Gulf countries, the UAE seems the most willing to offer immigrants citizenship. Elsewhere, nationality legally acquired, remains a closely guarded reward only offered for outstanding service to the state or to key political figures or exiles.

Dependence on migrants

Although the proportions of foreigners in the labour forces of the Gulf countries (Table 4.2) are an indication of a high degree of reliance on outside labour, the reciprocal relations which have developed between labour exporting and labour importing countries plus the diversity of sources of supply of labour mean that the Gulf countries are not as vulnerable to external forces as the employment figures would suggest. For many Middle Eastern countries the loss of workers' remittances would be a very serious problem (Table 4.3) so that there is a strong interest on the side of the labour exporters not to interfere dramatically with the supply of labour. In addition, when the Gulf countries have indicated that they can and will recruit workers, skilled and unskilled, from almost anywhere around the world, the chances of a sudden serious labour shortage developing are probably remote, although short term bottlenecks in the supply of particular grades of labour are more likely.

The real danger in depending on outside labour is not that the whole supply may suddenly dry up but that the workers themselves may cease to identify their interests with those of the state employing them and may combine or form associations aimed at furthering their own interests at the expense of the host country. This has not happened so far partly because of the prohibition of trade unions, and indeed almost all kinds of political activity in the Gulf, but also because of the high turnover rates of the immigrant labour forces. Only the longer established, semi-stable populations such as the Palestinians in Kuwait are at all likely to try to air their collective grievances but the external and internal policies in every Gulf state are strongly influenced by the need to prevent this kind of event happening. The strongly pro-PLO international stance of Kuwait is a direct outgrowth of the powerful position occupied by the Palestinians in the state. The balance is not an easy one to strike but the lack of major protests against the immigration or naturalization policies

of the labour importers and the discrimination system within the Gulf
countries is an indication that the governments have become skillful at
managing the situation. It is also a measure of the strength of the self-
interest shared by all immigrant workers in the Gulf who generally want
to continue earning money at existing rates in preference to trying to
change the system and possibly losing all. Quite deliberately, the Gulf
states set out to protect themselves by diversifying their sources of
labour supply so that difficulties with one country or group of countries
need not be a catastrophic blow. The trend towards the use of Asian
labour is notable in this context for the size of the pool from which the
Gulf countries can draw is virtually inexhaustible once the principle of
using non-Arab labour is established.

Table 4.2

Employment in selected Gulf countries around 1975

	Economically active nationals ('000)	Crude labour force participation rate (%)	Economically active aliens ('000)	Labour force aliens (%)
Bahrain	45.8	21.4	30.0	39.6
Kuwait	91.8	19.4	211.4	69.7
Oman	141.5	25.0	73.5	34.0
Qatar	12.5	18.4	53.8	81.1
Saudi Arabia	1,326.1	22.3	391.2	49.4
UAE	45.0	22.5	296.5	86.8

Source: Birks and Sinclair (1978, 1979)

Table 4.3

Flow of workers' remittances and its share in total imports and exports of goods in selected labour exporting countries

Country	1974 Remittances*	1974 As percentage of Exports	1974 As percentage of Imports	1975 Remittances	1975 As percentage of Exports	1975 As percentage of Imports	1976 Remittances	1976 As percentage of Exports	1976 As percentage of Imports	1977 Remittances	1977 As percentage of Exports	1977 As percentage of Imports
Algeria	390	9	9	466	11	7	245	5	4	246	4	3
Bangladesh ***	36	13	2	35	9	1	36	10	1	83	18	9
Egypt	189	11	5	367	23	7	754	47	18	1,425	66	27
India ***	276	8	5	490	12	8	750**	17	12	–	–	38
Jordan	75	48	12	167	109	18	396	198	34	425	186	38
Morocco	356	21	17	533	35	18	548	43	16	577	44	18
Pakistan ***	151	15	6	230	22	8	353	31	12	1,118	88	40
Syrian Arab Republic	62	8	4	55	6	3	51**	5	2	–	–	–
Tunisia	118	13	9	146	17	8	135	17	8	142	16	8
Turkey	1,425	93	33	1,317	94	25	982	50	17	982	56	17
Yemen Arab Republic****	159	1,325	69	221	1,556	72	525	4,269	137	1,013	5,449	139
Yemen PDR	41	410	23	56	373	32	115	261	40	179****	352	49

Sources: IMF consolidated balance of payments and World Bank Reports

– Data not available

* In current prices, million dollars, gross figures

** Estimate

*** Fiscal year ending June of the indicated year

**** Preliminary

71

It is possible for the pact between immigrants and nationals to break down. For example, a series of unfairly restrictive policies might force all migrant workers to combine against the government to obtain better working conditions and basic rights. Importation of cheaper Asian labour could create unrest amongst the traditional Arab sources of labour. These difficulties are never far below the surface; the replacement in recent months of Yemeni workers in Saudi Arabia by Asian, especially Pakistani labour, has led to return migration to North Yemen and to feelings of resentment on both sides. Clearly, it is only the constant monitoring and manipulation of the situation by the Gulf countries coupled with the vested interests of the workers which stands between order and chaos in the Gulf labour markets.

There is a secondary aspect of dependency which in the short run may be more important. This is the tendency to rely on a few sending countries for labour of a certain quality since, generally speaking, the labour exporting countries each specialize in the supply of migrants with particular levels of education and skills. Certain key sectors of the economy of each of the Gulf states are dominated by expatriates from just a few countries. In Kuwait, for example, 30 per cent of the school teachers in 1975 were from Jordan and Palestine and 32 per cent were from Egypt, although steps are being taken to reduce this dependency. Over two-thirds of all doctors and dentists were from the same two countries whereas almost half of all the tailors in Kuwait were from Pakistan. In Qatar, the civil service is heavily dependent on the northern Arab countries and Egypt, whereas almost all the traders and labourers in the private sector came from India, Pakistan and Iran. In Oman there is an especially heavy reliance on Asian labour in the building trades—carpenters, bricklayers, electricians, and also foremen and supervisors. In Saudi Arabia it is again the construction industry which uses the highest proportions of Asian labour plus dwindling numbers from North Yemen, but the commerce and personal services sector of the economy is also heavily dependent on Asians and to a lesser extent on northern area Arabs.

Despite all this foreign labour, the key policy decisions are still taken by nationals. In most Gulf countries an inner group of able and well educated nationals, often related to the ruling family, operate as an oligarchy and ensure that the running of the state remains firmly under the control of its citizens. It is this group of men who decide immigration and indeed all other policies. In the smaller states there is no well organized opposition to this 'junta' type of administration and the little that has emerged in the past (e.g. in the prorogued Kuwait National Assembly) has been suppressed. It seems that massive improvements in material welfare are sufficient at least to mute political opposition in the smaller Gulf states where divisions within the natural population are not as significant as in Iraq, Iran or even Saudi Arabia.

72

The Kuwait experience

The growth and change of the immigrant community is most fully documented in Kuwait where non-Kuwaitis (immigrants) grew from just 93,000 in 1957 to a total of 523,000 in 1975. Kuwait began its post-oil experience with an immigrant community drawn very largely from neighbouring countries—Iraq, Iran, Saudi Arabia and, to a lesser extent, from Oman and the Indian sub-continent. Initially a population of young unaccompanied males, the immigrant population has matured and changed until it has become more like the native population in age and sex composition (Table 4.4).

Table 4.4

Selected attributes of the immigrant population of Kuwait 1957–75

	Total non-Kuwaitis ('000)	Sex ratio	Under age 5 (%)	Males 10+ illiterate (%)
1957	92.8	365	7	43
1961	159.7	267	12	–
1965	247.3	236	15	33
1970	391.3	166	17	32
1975	522.7	143	17	27

Source: 1957, 1961, 1965, 1970 and 1975 censuses

Some of these compositional changes were due to the changing nationality structure of the non-Kuwaiti population (Table 4.5). In recent years the immigrants from the Gulf region have declined in proportional importance (although increasing in number) while the northern area Arabs (especially Jordanians and Palestinians) constitute an enlarged proportion of the total. The 'socio-economic status scale' groups together immigrants with similar levels of education, employment status and socio-economic activity. Thus, at one extreme, we find the Iranis, Omanis and Yemenis, over 83 per cent of whom have no schooling, with sex ratios over 555 and working in manual jobs or in sales and service activities. By contrast, Egyptians, Indians and Pakistanis are better educated, have more balanced sex ratios (133–179), work in professional, technical and clerical posts and are frequently accompanied by their wives and families. Other nationalities have intermediate positions on the simple typology which nevertheless captures some of the considerable variety within the non-Kuwaiti population.

Table 4.5

The national composition of the non-Kuwaiti population 1957—75

Nationality	1957 (%)	1965 (%)	1970 (%)	1975 (%)
Iraqi	28	10	10	9
Iranian	21	12	10	8
Jordanian and Palestinian	16	31	38	39
Lebanese	7	8	6	5
Omani	7	8	4	1
Indian	4	5	4	6
Pakistani	3	5	4	4
Saudi	2	4	2	2
Syrian	2	7	7	8
Egyptian	2	4	8	12
Others	8	9	7	6
Total (%'s)	100	100	100	100
Total numbers of non-Kuwaitis	92,851	247,280	391,266	522,749

Sources: Censuses of population 1957, 1965, 1970 and 1975, various tables

An additional point is that the number of non-Kuwaiti women in the labour force is very small (17 per cent) for an immigrant community and most of this proportion is accounted for by the Egyptian community which supplies Kuwait with most of its female school teachers (girls and boys are taught separately in Kuwait). Thus it seems that the attraction of Kuwait for potential migrants is twofold. Firstly, for young men it offers well paid employment together with some additional benefits like free medical care, some subsidized foodstuffs and sanitary housing. Secondly, for dependants, the attractions also include the availability of free schooling, cheap public utilities and access to a selection of goods (such as radios, clothing and cars) often unavailable or inaccessible because of their price or their scarcity in the home country.

Saudi Arabia, North Yemen and the Asian connection

Some estimates of the volume of Arab workers in the oil states have been collected by Birks and Sinclair and a summary of their findings is shown as Table 4.6. The importance of Saudi Arabia as a labour importer shows up clearly, but apart from some data on the nationality composition of the labour force (Table 4.7), we know very little about the size and recent changes in the non-Saudi population.

The country most affected by Saudi policies on immigration is North Yemen since Yemenis still constitute about one-third of the total labour force (over one-third of all foreign workers) in the kingdom. The effect of emigration and remittances on the North Yemeni economy is far reaching because of the size of the numbers involved and because almost all parts of the country have been touched by the exodus. Accurate meaurement of the number of Yemenis in Saudi Arabia is not easy but, by early 1980, we can estimate the total numbers of Yemenis abroad on a short term basis at about 575,000 (about 550,000 employed workers) with possibly another 175,000 longer term migrants. Not all work in Saudi Arabia but, using the same proportions by country as for the February 1975 census, we obtain a figure for all long and short term emigrants from Yemen in Saudi Arabia of just under 600,000. Of this total about 540,000 would be male workers.

These are crude estimates based on a revision of published statistics known to understate illegal cross border movements. Since 1975, several developments have occurred which will probably reduce the inflow of new migrants from Yemen. Firstly, the Yemeni government prohibited further emigration and restricted the issue of new passports. In 1978 Saudi Arabia also insisted on passports and work permits for Yemenis as for other nationalities. These slowed the rate of immigration but the determined migrant can simply walk across an unpatrolled section of the border or enter using a *hajj* visa. In November 1979 the raid on Mecca in which a North Yemeni tribal group near the Saudi border were heavily implicated resulted in deportations of Yemenis and Egyptians plus some other nationals.

The Yemeni community in Saudi Arabia is as varied in origin and experience as the Yemeni population itself. Many of the early Yemeni migrants to Saudi obtained experience in commerce, domestic service and other trades in Aden before 1967. This probably explains the very heavy out migration from the southern governorates of Ta'izz and Ibb where in certain districts 10–20 per cent of the total population or up to one-third of all men are working abroad. Men from Asir in the north find it easy to cross into the southern part of Sa'nosi where they are often seen as taxi drivers and construction workers. Some significant minorities from South Yemen are also part of the Yemeni community in Saudi—a good example are the religious leaders and goldsmiths from

Table 4.6

Arab migrant workers in the Middle East in 1975

Country of origin	Country of work								Total
	Bahrain	Iraq	Jordan	Kuwait	Libyan Arab Jamahiriya	Qatar	Saudi Arabia	United Arab Emirates	
Egypt	1,200	7,000	5,300	37,600	229,500	2,900	95,000	12,500	391,000
Iraq	100	–	–	18,000	–	–	2,000	500	20,600
Jordan (including Palestine)	600	5,000	–	47,700	14,200	6,000	175,000	14,500	263,000
Lebanon	100	3,000	7,500	5,700	500	20,000	20,000	4,500	48,500
Oman	1,400	–	–	3,700	–	1,500	17,500	14,000	38,100
People's Democratic Republic of Yemen	1,100	–	–	8,700	–	1,300	55,000	4,500	70,600
Somalia	–	–	–	200	–	–	5,000	1,000	6,200
Sudan	400	200	–	900	7,000	400	35,000	1,500	45,400
Syrian Arab Republic	100	–	20,000	16,500	13,000	800	15,000	4,500	69,000
Yemen Arab Republic	1,100	–	–	2,800	–	1,300	280,400	4,500	290,100
Maghreb	–	–	–	100	41,000	–	–	–	41,100
Total	6,100	15,200	32,800	143,400	310,400	14,700	699,900	62,000	1,284,500

– Indicates no migrants of this nationality recorded
Figures may not add due to rounding

Table 2.7

Employment by nationality in Saudi Arabia 1975

Nationality		Number ('000)	(%)
Saudi		1,026	57.1
N.Yemen		280	15.6
Jordanian and Palestinian		175	9.7
Egyptian		95	5.3
PDR Yemen		55	3.1
Sudan		35	1.9
Lebanese		20	1.1
Omani		17	0.9
Syrian		15	0.8
Somali		5	0.3
Iraqi		2	0.1
	Non-Saudi Arabs	700	38.9
Pakistani		15	0.8
Indian		15	0.8
Other Asian		8	0.4
	Asians	38	2.1
	Others	35	1.9
	Total non-Saudi	773	43.0
	Total	1,798	100.0

Sources: Labour Force Survey of Saudi Arabia and estimates by Birks and Sinclair (1979)

the Hadhramaut.

Certainly, any further tightening of Saudi controls on immigration and immigrants would affect North Yemen very profoundly. With only 2–3 per cent of imports covered by exports, Yemen's economy is kept afloat primarily by remittances, secondarily by aid. Private remittances quadrupled between 1972–73 and 1976–77 and further leaps more recently have sustained the development boom in more recent years. Despite the distorting affects of currently rapid inflation, Yemen would be in dire straits if remittances or Saudi aid were to be significantly reduced.

Recent estimates[1] suggest that in early 1979 there were probably 800,000 Asians in the Middle East of whom the majority were from India (300,000) and Pakistan (350,000). Bangladesh, Korea and the Phillipines were the other major labour exporters. These numbers are increasing steadily especially in the Gulf and Saudi Arabia as a result of the Mecca raid. Clearly, Saudi policy on import of labour is of central importance to a large number of Arab countries and to an increasingly large number of countries in Asia.

1 Keely, (1980), *Far Eastern Economic Review*, 1979.

Migrants and minorities in the larger Gulf countries

In Iraq and Iran temporary migrants have never been a major threat to the stability and independence of either country. In fact, it is very hard to see any link between demographic processes and the political fortunes of one or more of the tribal or religious groups which are so important in determining the longevity of the regimes in power. One can certainly imagine circumstances in which tensions could rise dangerously; the Gulf states, for example, could choose to exacerbate regional strains in Iran through these long established connections with Iranian immigrants from Baluchistan and Khuzistan. More likely is the possibility of further Iraq—Iran disagreement over Kurdistan and over the possibility of an 'Arabistan' in the south west of Iran. But these kinds of pressures are the result of foreign policy and not demography.

It may be useful to review briefly the main religious and ethnic groups present in each of the larger Gulf countries. Iraq has possibly the most heterogeneous native born population on the Arab side of the Gulf. The major split between Sunni and Shi'ia Islam was based on events which took place in what is now Iraq and so it is not surprising to find that about 55 per cent of the total population (three-quarters of the Arabs) are Shi'i Muslims. Despite attempts to overcome these sectarian differences by the 1958 Revolution and the 1964 Interim Constitution, the Shi'i heartland in Kut and Amara provinces in the south maintains its characteristic outlook. The 1958 land reform proved unsuccessful in the south, resulting in the 1961 Amara Laws which in some ways protected the rights of the Shi'i shaikhs. As a result, migration to Baghdad from the poverty stricken marsh area has been very significant and the largely illiterate Shi'i peasantry forms the bulk of the shanty-town population of eastern Baghdad.

North of Baghdad, the population is largely Sunni and this includes the dwindling Badu. By far the largest Sunni group are the Kurds who probably constitute 15–20 per cent of the total Iraqi population. As a group, the Kurds also spread over Syria, Turkey and Iran and probably number eight million in all, of whom about two million each are in Iraq and Iran. Far from unified, divided into three distinct linguistic and tribal groups (Badinan, Suran and Baban), the history of Kurdish resistance to central control is long and well studied. Again, the issue is how strongly one or more outside forces encourage the Kurds in the pursuit of the Kurdistan ideal.

Without introducing the less important minorities such as the Turkomans, the Persians, Lurs, Yezidis, Christians and Mandeans, it is plain that the oil wealth of Iraq has not made the government or development of this complicated country any easier. Despite investment by the state in agriculture and heavy industry, substantial parts of the Iraqi population are not part of the modern economy and it is inevitable that

78

some groups will want to redistribute the national cake in their favour, particularly as the cake is seen as not only large and tempting but also as unequally sliced.

Saudi society is by contrast much more homogeneous although the tide of immigration has swept in a largely Arab population of 'wage slaves'. For most political purposes, these non-Saudis are not seen as a major threat to the regime since they are 'disenfranchised' and have vested interests compatible with those of the Saudi rulers. Much more of a threat are the immigrants from neighbouring countries in which one or more revolutions have politicized the population. Some immigrants from both Yemens, Somalia, Sudan and even Egypt fall into this category, and the Shi'i oil workers of Iranian descent in eastern Arabia may be added to this list. The vulnerability of the regime to irredentism, especially with a religious twist, was demonstrated in November 1979 when the Shi'ia population became politically restive and were dealt with firmly by the Saudi authorities.

Of all the Gulf countries, Iran is probably the most complex and much of this complexity stems from the tribal and ethnic variety within its borders. From a demographic standpoint all that can be done here is to indicate the magnitude of the differentials in population growth and welfare which exist in Iran. Whilst in urban areas fertility was falling and infant mortality was no more than 60 per thousand, in rural areas fertility was virtually unchanged (crude birth rates of around 50 per thousand) and infant mortality at least 120 per thousand in the mid 1970s. Much wider differentials can be found within a single city but perhaps the most useful conclusion from the available statistics is that different groups and different parts of the country have had very different experiences under the Shah. As in most developing countries, income and welfare differentials initially widen before closing again as the state machinery for redistribution improves. The strains during the critical middle phase can be disastrous for the ruling authorities.

The political response to immigration and rapid population growth

Several of the well established immigrant groups in Arabia assert quite accurately that without their help the Arab oil exporting countries would not be where they are today. It is remarkable that this sentiment has received little political expression and that the host populations have managed to preserve their dominant position despite, in many cases, being a minority group in their own country. Some of the reasons for this have been explained above but it may be valuable to summarize here the main features of the system which allows the nationals to continue to exercise a considerable degree of control over their immigrant populations.

Legal provisions for control of entry

The six Arabian oil exporters have enacted very similar legislation which provides for:

1 Entry visas required for all visitors.

2 The sponsorship and responsibility for workers being assumed by employers.

3 The issue of work permits and entry visas outside the country of immigration.

4 Annual renewal of all work permits and visas.

5 Deportation by administrative order rather than by legal proceedings.

Nationality laws

In most states, these provide for:

1 Witholding of naturalization from most immigrants, even long established residents, and those born in the country of residence.

2 Witholding of full rights of citizenship for some period of years or forever from those newly naturalized.

Labour laws

The preference system for nationals is protected by laws stating:

1 Nationals must be offered a job opening first, followed by other Arabs and lastly all other foreigners.

2 Certain kinds of job, e.g. senior civil service positions, jobs in the army and police and even jobs such as driving a taxi, are reserved for nationals.

3 immigrants are not paid fully for some of the welfare benefits due to nationals (benefits include cash payments for family support, rent subsidies, pensions, etc.).

Property and business laws

The laws on these topics are extensive and complex but in general they state that:

1 Only citizens can own outright land, buildings and businesses.

2 Foreign participation in a businessmust be less than a majority shareholding.

3 Immigrants are excluded from the subsidized housing which is a feature of all the Gulf states and also from the property compensation schemes through which governments pass huge sums of money to the people.

4 Commercial licences for trade including importing all restricted to nationals.

Political activities

The governments generally prohibit:

1 Most forms of criticism of the government and its policies.

2 All parties, organizations or trade unions are prohibited unless especially approved (e.g. the Bahrain Family Planning Association had to obtain special permission to open more than a headquarters office).

3 Public demonstrations, strikes, political protests, etc.

This very general summary indicates the nature of the legal controls at the disposal of the governments of the region to control immigration and the immigrants, but there are in addition a number of standard practices which further circumscribe the rights of foreign workers. One of the implications of the laws on ownership of property and businesses is that only certain residential areas contain accommodation for renting. Thus a system of residential segregation exists in most cities. As a corollary, the services in the immigrant areas are less well developed and facilities such as the health clinics and the co-operative shopping centres in the housing areas designed for nationals are not accessible to non-residents. The immigrant housing areas are often crowded and dirty compared to the luxurious living conditions of the national population. In their daily life, therefore, immigrants of all nationalities are constantly reminded of their inferior status.

A second implication of the laws on immigration is that it is possible to discriminate against certain nationalities by simply refusing them entry and work permits. Thus, groups who might be inclined to settle with their dependants can be prevented from entering or even forced to leave at the annual review of permits. At any time a national can insist on obtaining the job of an immigrant, resulting in the displacement of that immigrant. Thus, when the school system finds it difficult to keep up the provision of teachers and classrooms, it is the immigrant children who are excluded from public schools and whose parents may face increasing difficulty in renewing their work and residence permits.

Viewed *in toto,* the collection of laws coupled with extensions to the laws by 'usual practice' amounts to a comprehensive set of controls designed to make full use of immigrant labour whilst conceding only the bare minimum to the immigrants in the way of civil rights, welfare benefits and naturalization possibilities. Clearly, the attractive salaries offered and the self-interest and conservatism they engender are the prime factors preventing political pressures for the improvement in the position of the foreign workers from developing a powerful momentum.

Conclusion

The main population related problem faced by the oil exporting countries of Arabia is the control of immigration and the immigrant communities they employ. Over the years the governments of the Gulf states have considered proposals for the naturalization of many of the long stay immigrants but this seems an unlikely policy change in present circumstances. One of the results of very rapid natural increase rates of the national populations is that the nationals feel slightly more secure now that their numbers are at least into six figures and approaching seven. The Kuwaitis, for example, were quite pleased to find they had at least a million people in the state by the time the 1975 census results were announced.

Since wholesale naturalization of sizeable parts of the immigrant communities is unlikely in the foreseeable future, it is fair to ask about the meaning of the kinds of development now under way in the Gulf states. Some figures from Kuwait illustrate this point very well: taking the book values of the assets of ten joint stock companies in Kuwait and their employment of Kuwaitis, we find that each Kuwaiti job represents an investment of at least £75,000. Admittedly, the Kuwaitis were probably the senior management but this kind of development of capital intensive, high technology industries often connected to the downstream end of the oil industry provide very few employment prospects for the bulk of the Kuwaiti population, not all of whom are millionaires. In these circumstances, and despite the regional benefits which flow from the remittance income of migrants, it is difficult to escape the conclusion that for the long term stability of the Gulf countries and for the improvement of the quality of life of all the national populations, not just the well educated elites, it is necessary for them to re-think their investment and development programmes and at the same time to encourage more of their nationals to participate at all levels in operating their own economies.

Notes

The majority of the demographic estimates were derived from original sources but the following sources were also referred to and quoted in places:

Benham, D. and Amani, M., *La Population de l'Iran*, CICRED Monographic Series, 1974.

Courbage, Y. and Kjurciev, A., 'Alternative population projections and analysis of the essential data in Bahrain', *ECWA Population Bulletin*, 6, January 1974.

Hill, A.G., 'The demography of the population in Kuwait', *Demography*, 12, 3, 537–548, 1975.

Levels and Trends in Fertility and Mortality in Kuwait, University of Jordan and the US National Academy of Sciences, 1979.

Iran, Plan and Budget Organization, *Population Growth of Iran, First Survey Year 1973–74*, 1976.

UN ECWA (Beirut) (Annual) *Population Data Sheets*.

Many of the statistics on immigration come from a series produced by Birks, J.S. and Sinclair, C.A. as part of their international migration study at Durham University. The main country reports are:

Kuwait 1977, Oman 1977, Qatar 1978, UEA 1978, Bahrain 1978, Saudi Arabia 1979.

The laws on international migration in the region have been reviewed by Georges Dib:

Migration and naturalization laws in the Arab Republic of Egypt, the Hashemite Kingdom of Jordan, Kuwait, Lebanon, the Syrian Arab Republic and the United Arab Emirates, paper for the UN ECWA Seminar on Population and Development, Amman, 18–30 November 1978, E/ECWA/POP/WG.12/BP.5 and in a paper on the same topic for a seminar in Washington DC in 1979.

Many of the ideas on international migration in the Middle East were discussed at a study group sponsored by the Population Council at the Jordanian Royal Scientific Society in December 1978. The key paper was presented by Charles B. Keely. See *Report on the Study Group on Migration Abroad*, Amman, Population Council WANA Regional Paper, 2–3 December 1978. The information on North Yemen comes from an anthropology fieldworker there, Ms Cynthia Myntti of the London School of Economics. The two stage model of immigration is evaluated in:

Hill, A.G., 'Les travailleurs etrangers dans les pays du Golf', *Tiers-Monde*, 18, 69, 115–13, 1977.

See also Charles B. Keely's paper on 'Asian Worker Migration to the Middle East', Population Council, Centre for Policy Studies, Working Paper 52, 1980.

Index

Abdul Aziz, Sa'ud Ibn, 2, 4, 14, 16

Abu Dhabi: armed forces of, 23, 24; assistance to other members of UAE, 21; basis data on, 57; coup of 1966, 4; distribution of wealth in, 50; conflict with Dubai, xi; jealousy of Dubai, 27–8; equity participation in oil industry, 24; gas industry of, 49; infrastructure development of, 41–3; investments of, 41–2; and Iran, 21; oil industry participation, 24; oil output ceiling, 39; Palestinians in, 67; Shakhbut deposed, 4; dispute with Saudi Arabia, 19, 21; and UAE federal powers, 22; possible withdrawal from UAE, 35

Abu Dhabi city, 28

Afghanistan: invaded by USSR, viii

agents: limit on commission of, 52

agriculture: decline in, 63

'Ajman, 21, 23, 35

al-Khatib, Dr Ahmed, 8

Algeria: workers' remittances to, 71

Algiers Accord, 21n

amir (commander): evolution of role of, 3; as title, 2

Atiqu, Abdel-Rahman, 38, 54

Bahrain: basic data on, 56, 76; budget introduced in, 3; constitutional development of, xii, 1–5, 6–7; distribution of wealth in, 50; diversification in 42, 48, 65; employment data, 70; government in, 1–5, 6–7; Haraka in, 6; immigrant population of, 7, 76; infrastructure development in, 41–3; Nasserism in, 6; national economy of, 48; oil production decline, 7, 39; oil production and societal change, x, 39, 64–5; parliament in, 6–7; as regional

Haraka (Movement of Arab Nationalists): in Bahrain, 6; in Kuwait, 8; on privilege, 8
health and social services: finance for, 52; and immigrants, 32, 33
housing: differences in, 63—4; segregation of citizens and immigrants, 63; schemes, 51

ideology: as source of conflict, ix
immigrants: amnesty for, 31; Asian, 62—3, 70, 72; in Bahrain, 7; as cause of conflict, x, xi; control of, 66, 67—8, 79—82; data for each oil producing state, 56—7; discrimination policy against, 68—9, 80—1; economic function of, 43—4, 52—3, 59, 64, 69—72, 75—6, 79; education of, 31—2, 33, 79; fertility of, 61; health and social services for, 32, 80, 81; illegal, 31, 66, 75; increase in, 58, 61—2; in Kuwait, x, xi, 8, 10—11, 11, 56, 68, 69—70, 70, 72, 73—4; Palestinian, 11; pattern of and oil development, 64—5, 66; as proportion of labour force, 69, 70; quotas on, 67—8; remittances from, 71; residential segregation of, 63—4, 81; in Saudi Arabia, x, xi, 14, 15; and Saudi Arabian industrial development, 43—4, 59, 64; in structure of society, 11, 79—82; transient or permanent, 32—3; in UAE, xi, 30 —4
imports, reliance on, 63
India: migrants to Middle East from, 77; political responsibility for Gulf states, 65; workers' remittances to, 71
industrialisation, 38
industry: and environment, 46;

heavy, 43—5; and labour supply, 63; light, 45—7; loans for, 45, 52; service, 42
infrastructure: development of, 41—3
investment, 41—2, 82
Iran: claims to Bahrain, 7; economic malaise in, 53—4; foreign workers in, 59; gas in, 49; housing conditions in, 63—4; immigrants from, 62; investments of, 41; land reform in, 64; migrants in, 76—7; modernisation of, xi; population decline in, 59; religious and ethnic groups of, 79; revolution in, ix, xi, 7; secret service in, 17; and Sharjah, 27; and UAE, 19, 21, 21n
Iraq: offered support to Bahrain against Iran, 7; constitutional development in, xii; foreign workers in, 59; housing conditions in, 63—4; immigrant population of, 76; and Kuwait, 13; and land reform in, 64; migrant workers of, 76, 78—9; religious and ethnic groups of, 79—80; and UAE, 19, 21, 21n
Islamic code: rules of in Saudi Arabian society, 15
Israel: as factor in migration pattern to Gulf states, 65; Western support for and Gulf states, ix

Jordan: immigrant population of, 76; migrant workers of, 76; workers' remittances to, 71

Khawarij, 16
Khor Fakkan, 28—9
Kuwait: army of, 13; basic data on, 56, 73—4, constitutional

development, xii, 1—5; corporation tax, 51—2; data on non-Kuwaiti population, 73—4, 76; distribution of wealth in, 50, 51, 52—3, 54; diversification in, 42; employment data, 72; expatriates in, 72; government, 1—5; history of, 8—13, immigrants, x, xi, 8, 10—11, 56, 68, 68—9, 70, 72, 73—4; infrastructure developed in, 41 —3; investments of, 41—2; Iraqi threat, 13; loans to light industry in, 45; military expenses of, 13; nationalisation of Kuwait Oil Co., 8; naturalisation policy, 68—9; oil production and society in, x; oil output ceiling, 39—40; Palestinians in, 8, 9, 12, 61, 65, 67, 69; parliament in, 8, 9—10; professional groups in, 10—11; social welfare in, 11—12; structure of society in, 11—13, 17; teachers in, 72, 74

Kuwait Oil Co: nationalised, 8

labour force: Asians in, 62—3, 70; control of flow of, 66, 67—8; make-up of, 69—70; remittances of immigrants, 71; in Saudi Arabia, 48; source of, 62, 69, 70; in UAE, 33—4; and women, 64

land: as means of distributing wealth in Kuwait, 51; as gift in Saudi Arabia, 51; ownership restrictions, 51, 63, 66, 80; reform, 64

Lebabon: migrant workers of, 78

Libyan Arab Jamahiriya: immigrant population of, 76

Majlis, 2, 3

Maghreb: migrant workers of, 76

Malik, (King), 2

manual labour: aversion to, 34, 39, 48

marriage: role of multiple in Saudi Arabian society, 14

Mecca: conquest of by Abdul Aziz, 2; Great Mosque occupied, 16, 53

modernisation: as source of conflict, x, xi

Morocco: workers'remittances to 71

mortality, 58

Moslem religion: role of in Saudi Arabian society, 14—15, 17, *see also* Shi'i, Sunni

'Muslim revival', 53

Nasser, Abdul, 4, 16

Nasserism: in Bahrain, 6; in Saudi Arabia, 4

naturalisation, 68—9, 80, 82

OAPEC (Organisation of Arab Petroleum Exporting Countries): dry dock, 63

OECD (Organisation for Economic and Cultural Development): dependency on Gulf oil, xiii, ix

OPEC (Organisation of Petroleum Exporting Countries): UAE versus Saudi Arabia in 1976, 25

oil: Arab states dependence on, 38—40; conservation of, 42; data for each oil producing state, 56—7; development of society, ix, 12; embargoes, ix; government participation in industry, 24; income versus spending, 39; OECD dependency on Gulf for, viii; output ceilings on, 39—40; population growth and, 61, 64—5;

price, ix, 39—40; rate of production, ix; security of supply and politicisation, xii—xiii, 12

Oman: basic data, 57; coup of 1970, 4; distribution of wealth in, 50; Dhofar rebellion, 21; employment data, 70; expatriates in, 72; immigrants from, 62; infrastructure development in, 41—3; migrant workers of, 76; oil production decline, 39; Taimour deposed, 4; and UAE, 19

PDRY (Peoples Democratic Republic of Yemen); migrant workers of, 76; return of migrants to, 62, 72; workers' remittances to, 71

PFLOAG (Peoples Front for the Liberation of Oman and the Arab Gulf), 4

Pakistan: migrants from to Middle East, 77; workers' remittances to, 71; workers in Saudi Arabia, 72

Palestinians: in Abu Dhabi, 67; Arab League decision on naturalisation of, 68; fertility levels of, 61; in Kuwait, 8, 9, 10, 11, 12, 67, 69; naturalisation of, 68; in Saudi Arabia, 14, 67; as source of labour, 62, 65

Patriotic Club of Kuwait, 10

politicisation: and outside cultural influences, 53; and security of oil supply, xii—xiii

Popular Democratic Front (Hawatmeh), 11

Popular Front (Habash), 11

population: data for each oil producing state, 56—7; and development of oil industry, 61; female education and control of increases in, 61; growth of, x, 58, 59, 60; mix and political alignments, 65; political use of in emirates, 22; problems of, 59; in urban areas, 63; see also immigrants

prime minister: as successor to 'throne', 3

professional classes: in Kuwait, 10

profit controls, 54, 55

Qatar: basic data on, 57; constitutional development, 4—5; distribution of wealth in, 50; diversification in, 48, 65; employment data, 70; expatriates in, 72; gas, 49; immigrant population of, 76; infrastructure development in, 41—3; investments of, 41—2; oil production decline, 39, 48; road to Europe, 12

Ra's al-Khaymah, 19, 21, 22, 30

Rashid, Shaikh: accepts UAE premiership, 29, 36; extends term of office, 35; support for UAE, 22

religion: as cause of conflict, 59

rents: as source of private income, 39

rural—urban drift, 53—4, 54, 65, 66

Saudi Arabia: dispute with Abu Dhabi, 19, 21; agricultural development in, 54; aid to other UAE states, 40; army of, 18; Asian immigrants in, 65; Bahraini parliament, 6; basic data on, 56; role of Bedouin of, 14, 15, 17; constitutional development, xii, 1—5; distribution of wealth, 50, 51—2; electricity tariff cut in, 54; employment data, 72; expatriates in, 74; occupation of Great Mosque of Mecca, 16, 75, 77, 79; immigrant control, 68; immigrant population of, x, xi, 14, 15, 59, 72, 75–7; industrial routine in, 48; infrastructure development in, 41–3; labour importing policy, 75–7; loans to light industry in, 45–6; multiple marriage in, 14, 16–17; Nasserism, 4; North Yemeni workers in, 72, 75; oil production and society of, x; oil output ceilings, 39–40; oil revenue impact, 14; Pakistani workers in, 72; Palestinians in, 14, 67; use of religion in society, 14–15, 17, 79, religions and ethnic groups in, 79; religious riots in, 53; rural –urban drift in, 54; Shi'i activity, 75, 79; role of Secret Service in, 17; structure of society in, 12–13, 14–17, 17–18; support for UAE, xi, 21, 22

SIDF (Saudi Industrial Development Fund), 45

secret service: in Iran, 17; in Saudi Arabia, 17

segregation, residential: caused by restrictions on land ownership, 63

Shah of Iran, 7, 16, 23, 40

shaikh: system of government by, 1–5

Sharjah: boundary dispute with Dubai, 27; boundary dispute with Fujayrah, 27; boundary dispute with Umm al-Qaywayh, 27; commercial development of, 28–9; and independent statehood, 30; jealousy of Dubai, 28; territorial claims of, 19

Shi'i: and Arab collaboration, 8; claims to Bahrain, 7; and revolution in Iran, 7; in Iraq, 78; in Saudi Arabia, 16, 75, 77, 79

Six Day War, 4

smuggling, 42

social security, 51, 54

social welfare: and immigrants, 66; in Kuwait, 11–12

Somalia: migrant workers of, 76

standard of living, 50

Straits of Hormuz, 29

students: in UAE, 31–2

Sudan: immigrants from, 64, 78

Sunni: in Iraq, 78; versus Shi'ites in Bahrain, 7

Syrian Arab Republic: migrant workers of, 76; workers' remittances to, 71

tariffs, 46

taxation, 38, 51–2, 54–5

telephone system, 52

territory: Haraka on, 8; as source of conflict, ix; problems of in UAE, 19, 26–7

trade unions: prohibited, 69, 81

tribal tradition: and constitutional development, 1–5; and multiple marriage in Saudi Arabia, 16–17; and removal of unfit rulers, 3–5

Tunisia: workers' remittances to, 71

Turkey: workers' remittances to, 71

UAE (United Arab Emirates), 19–38; Abu Dhabi's aid to other members, 21; administration for, 26; armed forces of, 23–4, 34; authority of ministries of, 30; border disputes, 26–7; conflict within, 25–30;

constitutional provisions of, 21;
creation of, 19; education and
federal government, 23, 24–5,
26, 31; employment data, 70;
ethnicity in, 32; expatriates in,
24–5, 32; future of, 35–7;
immigrant population, x, xi,
32–3, 76; immigration, 30–4,
industrial co-ordination in, 29
–30; information policies, 24;
internal frontiers of, 20; and
Iran, 21, 21n; and Iraq, 19, 21,
21n; naturalisation policy, 69;
oil production and societal
change, x–xi; population aug-
mentation in poor emirates,
22; realignment of, 29; and
Saudi Arabia, xi, 21; students
view of, 32; succession in, 27;
teachers in, 31; technology in,
27–9; territorial problems, 19
US: and Gulf states, viii; support
for UAE, 22
USSR: invasion of Afghanistan,
viii; interest in Gulf states, viii;
oil needs of, viii

Umm al-Qaywayn: dispute with
Sharjah, 27; leadership in 23;
and UAE, 21, 35
urbanisation, x, 65–6

violence: and immigrants in UAE,
32

Wahhabis, 14
water, cost of, 52
welfare policies, 52, 82
women: attitudes to, 64; education of and control of population, 61; role of, 64

YAR (Yemeni Arab Republic):
economy, 75, 77; migrant
workers of, 14, 75, 76; prohibition of emigration, 75;
return of migrants, 62, 72;
workers' remittances to, 71

zakat, 51
Zayid, Shaikh, 22, 24n, 25, 27,
35